# The Universe According To NOWMAN

Dan Nowman Niswander

# The Universe According To NOWMAN

**Dan Nowman Niswander**

nowmanrightnow1999@gmail.com

First edition
ISBN: 978-0-9886770-0-5

Library of Congress- United States Copyright Office
Registration Number: TXu 1-838-552

Edited, layout, and overall design by Daniel R. Niswander
Cover design and additional artwork by J Wander
Photography by Dan Nowman Niswander and Mil Bagul

Published by Daniel R. Niswander

Lyon's Den Productions


LD3- B1

**Preface**

What is the Universe?  NOW, that's a loaded question isn't it?
While many people, philosophers, teachers, and the like have asked and
discussed this question most likely since the advent of humankind on this
Earth planet, it continues to engage the inspired mind.

It is my hope that this book carefully considers the meaning of this topic of
unlimited content. Whether one reads this book in one period of time or little
bits at a time, I hope that it will make a lasting impression and perhaps be
utilized for moments of refreshment, contemplation, inspiration, and even
some humor along the path in this human Earth journey that we ALL share.

I leave this for you to interpret for yourself as you see fit because you are the
one who is consciously experiencing the so-called feelings and emotions, or
whatever it is that you feel or don't feel as you read this.  If you are confused
after reading this introduction or are uncertain concerning what this book is
actually about, the last sentence here may help you to understand more.

*Enjoy and always remember... All that exists is right NOW!*

Love and Peace,

Dan NOWMAN Niswander

## ABOUT THE AUTHOR

Dan Nowman Niswander (pronounced nice-wander) is a multi-media artist: a singer, songwriter, keyboardist, actor, entertainer, published writer, music and video producer, an entrepreneur, and a storyteller. He has even been president of a non-profit, a media ambassador, and an Internet reporter in a Hollywood press corps, is an occasional blogger, an activist, advocate for education, and more. He has Swiss ancestry, but doesn't play the accordion...yet.

He began singing at the age of 5 and playing the piano by the age of 10. His two albums of original music include the catchy pop, rock and funk songs "Fun (To the Nth Degree)," "Read A Book," "Hats," "Everyone," "Mojo," "Chameleon," "Funky Space," "Compassion," "Out of Order," and "Surfin' With Jesus," some which have received radio airplay. The first professional gig as a composer landed him soundtrack credits in an infomercial in Hollywood and his music has also been featured in a promotional film "Chameleon" that he also co-produced and it was screened at a midwestern film festival. As a musician and entertainer, he has performed in and hosted thousands of shows in the Midwest to California and from 2001 to 2004, he produced and hosted a popular local live monthly variety show in Indianapolis, Indiana. His music has been featured on FM band commercial and also Internet radio stations. He and his band have performed live on local television in Indianapolis.

He has earned a Bachelor's degree in Business Administration-Marketing.

As an actor, he has created approximately a dozen 'Rock Theater' characters that have been featured in audio recordings, video productions, and numerous live shows, and has appeared in independent films such as the award winning independent film 'Saving Star Wars" and webisodes even appearing with actor Jason Alexander.

Besides music, he has also produced video shorts and music videos.

His extensive print coverage includes being named Best Showman and has also appeared on the front page of a major newspaper.

As a writer, his articles have been featured in various publications. He has conducted, gathered, and produced interviews with a diversity of people including Beatle Paul McCartney, Hollywood celebrities such as Jay Leno, Mickey Rooney, Buddy Ebsen, and Cindy Williams, other musicians, actors, and even writers and activists.

(More information follows the search guide at the rear of the book)

There are always so many people that I can thank and too many to literally list here. Some of you have been given thanks in the packaging of my music albums so some of you know who you are. The only way to not leave anyone out is to say first of all **THANK YOU TO EVERYONE and the UNIVERSE** which is everything and everyone anyhow!

This book is dedicated to my father Robert (whom many of his friends called brother Bob) and also to my dear friends Jon Withrow and Joh Padgett, and to another incredibly talented musician Charlie Smith that I had the privilege to work with, all who left the Earth experience early. I know they are still somewhere in the Universe... NOW!

**THIS BOOK DRAWS INSPIRATION FROM AND GIVES SPECIAL THANKS TO** my parents Robert and Martha that taught how most importantly love and loyalty is, my ultra talented biological brother Joe, my adventurous Swiss grandparents Ernst and Lidia that came across Ellis Island to find opportunity and after severe hardship, settled down in a village called Independence inspiring me more and more even though they are no longer on this Earth planet, Fellow Syndicate Gentlemen Clark Davis, Fernando Garces and Xaime Casillas, one of my Spiritual brothers Mikal Kamil, all of my friends at Occupy (too many to mention) including original Occupy Wall Street organizer David DeGraw, my friends George, Mark J., Stephen, Mary Beth, Anna, Anthony, and all from the intelligence collective of the commons and the Future of Occupy in London and around the world, the 99% and the 1% who get it, Brian Ray, Andrew, Mike, Howard, Heather, Jonni, Jay, and ALL of my family at Ground Control that accepted me for who I am, Bernard B., Sean and the Hollywood Happiness Club, Mark D., Mil, Uthra, Emman, Rondell, Rik, Ray, Jeff, Jose, Rory, and all of the Trader Joes friends, Pete, Jeff C., Elle, Pam, Kim, David, Grace, Maria, Tony, Al, Lorena, Maria, Gevork, Erica, Lynn, Abran, Carol, Elizabeth, Jesse, Azad, also Paddy H., and Tom from the Light Bringer Project and the Doo Dah Parade, El, Mindy, Arthur, Abel, and all current and so-called future friends of NOWMAN wherever you are in the Universe...EVERYONE...HERE and NOW!

Cheers,
Dan

## THE STORY OF NOWMAN:

## WHERE FACT SEEMS TO MEET FICTION AND FANTASY SEEMS TO MEET REALITY

Once upon a time a regular guy, who is a journalist, has a revelation that the Universe is timeless and only exists in the NOW. He is hit by a cosmic ray and becomes NOWMAN, whose primary mission is to remind everyone that he comes in contact with that the past is gone, the future is yet to come, and it is NOW!

Who is NOWMAN? Is he a figment of your imagination? Is he human or merely a cartoon character in human form? Who is this mystery man superhero? Is he here to help save the world from the folly of living in the past or the future? NOWMAN is the superhero of each and every moment. His super powers include the ability to fly through the air like a bird, highly developed social skills, and the uncanny ability to keep his other powers secret until the time comes that he needs to use them. Apparently he does like the thrill of riding a surfboard on the ocean, playing vintage musical instruments, hosting shows, promoting good, wearing cheap sunglasses and the color of purple, oh, and I shall not forget, being a citizen journalist and integrative reporter. In any event, NOWMAN is here to serve by doing what is morally and ethically right while bringing the present moment up front and center in each encounter.

Whether as a citizen journalist or blogger, in a nightclub, on the street, a live concert, television broadcast, online webisodes, the front page of a major newspaper or website, at a festival, parade, art gallery opening, college or university campus, race track, a rally, and any other social scene or activity, or whenever spontaneity is apparent, NOWMAN is ready to respond as the need arises.

NOWMAN is the new superhero in town!

As his theme song 'Fun (To the Nth Degree)' states…. "The past is gone, the future is yet to come. It's NOW. RIGHT NOW! The present is here, the future is near, but it's right now… HERE NOW !

## AN INTRODUCTION FROM *NOWMAN*

Before leaping into this book, this introduction is being written because I feel that it appropriately sets the vibe and the tone of what you are about to read. It comes first from a place of LOVE.

1. Keep on loving each other

(helping each other, individually doing what's right, doing what's best for everyone, keeping the ego in check always, keeping it real!)

2. Keep on raising awareness

(educating each other, connecting with each other especially face to face, being reliable and fair, engaging more and more with others in deeper more meaningful ways even through social media no matter where you are in the Universe)

3. Keep on engaging peaceful progress

(stay focused on priorities, expanding your horizons, planning always starts NOW even when something seems to be happening later)

SOME TIPS BEFORE READING THIS BOOK: The language in this book is primarily written from the standpoint of Universal perspective because consciousness and conscious living is much more than the Earth or the human experience. With this in mind, the human experience sees the universe as dualistic, but the Universal perspective (I like the word Awareness better than perspective) sees only ONE Conscious and complete Experience happening NOW in a non-linear spaceless and timeless continuum. In other words, you'll never find a line of demarcation around the Universe, but in the human experience, there are plenty of ways to try and put the Universe into a box or draw lines around it. The Universe is full of diversity, so that is why there are all kinds of subject matter. When I capitalize certain words (other than proper words such as Earth or Einstein, for example), I am pointing out the distinction between the human perception and the Universal perception. For instance, when I write the word 'love' I would be talking about the Earth experience of love: romantic, parental, platonic person to person, love of nature, etc. When I use the word

'Love' I am referring to something much greater that must be understood from the standpoint of the Universe that truly cannot really be understood

from a human perspective. This is exactly why words are a challenge sometimes. Of course all of this is in the context of the present moment because NOW is all that we are aware of this moment.

Remember, everyone can be a superhero... one way or another, keep your ego in check and have FUN doing all of that with whatever genuine good that you bring into this world.

Here and NOW,
NOWMAN

# 1. So What's New?

I am starting this book just like we start a calendar year.

We have this holiday called New Year's Day. It is celebrated in some way or another everywhere around the globe as far as we know…unless of course there is some undiscovered culture in the most remote portion of a tropical jungle or at the actual depths of the deepest ocean that just doesn't make that an important matter if that is even possible. We symbolically see it as the fresh start of life in some way; starting over or something like that. There is also a lot of talk about new years' resolutions.

But what really is new? We are still conscious as we were before the new year started. That is how it was last year, too, and the year before that, and the year before that, and the year before that and so on… you get my drift. Being conscious is constant so it isn't new.

So what is new then? Good question!
Perhaps what we pay attention to each moment is new and that is why I call each moment the Eternal NOW! Life seems to be an unlimited number of moments, but each one is still just the present experience.

What is a new years' resolution? Do I need to change the way that I am conscious? I don't think that's possible. I'm aware of being alive every waking moment so why would I need to try to change that? Maybe I need to change my attitude about something or change a bad habit to a good one or something like that. Hmmm. What if I don't actually follow through? Can I try again next year?

So what is the basic thought that I want to get across here?
Maybe that would be that nothing is actually new… maybe we just believe that we have to judge life as new or old or something in between.
I am just having a little fun here, but a familiar expression feels true to me…
*There's nothing new under the sun*

or anywhere else for that matter.

## 2. The Child's Perspective

A child has a unique perspective of the world which is actually its' experience of the Universe. The child doesn't know about many limitations or restrictions that the adult counterparts seem to experience, and is fascinated with the realm of discovery in every waking moment.

The adult's role should be to allow that discovery to unfold without unnecessary interference since the Universe Itself isn't restricted or limited. Just like what most parents would identify as discipline, there can be those moments where attention is needed to 'truly' help guide the child in a direction that keeps it from what could be called harm's way or chaotic circumstances. Now of course defining harm and chaos can be identified in as many ways as there are opinions about the definitions. The general idea is not to restrict but to leave the experiences of life discovery as open as possible.

This not only prepares a child for the years ahead, but more importantly allows the child the freedom to see more of what the Universe actually is.

The same principle applies to adults really. If we limit our experiences of the openness of the Universe, we seem to miss something. There is no possible way to actually put lines of demarcation or limitation around the Universe, so why even try?

It seems to me that the only motive for doing that or attempting to do that, aside from having good intentions at best, would be more about power and control over others than it would be the true benefit of the individual 'being' himself or herself without such impositions. The fulfillment of one's purpose in this so-called human experience is essential.

## 3. Fun (To the Nth Degree)

Fun is one of my favorite words. It is such a simple word with only 3 letters, one syllable, and so much deep content with a meaning that should be simple to understand.

Fun, as I see it, is true contentment mixed with the enjoyment of life. We do enjoy life thoroughly when we feel good inside and outside…emotionally, physically, mentally…. It all could be called Spiritual.

Living life to the Nth degree simply means living 'to the utmost,' am I right? Loving oneself and others to the Nth degree would mean loving 'to the utmost.' So… it would make sense to me that fun to the nth degree means enjoyment 'to the utmost.'
This is one of my primary philosophies in this life.

## 4. What is NOW?

**NOW** is what is the focus of our attention in the present moment. There really isn't past because it seems to be gone and there really isn't future because that is speculation at this point. Even when we think about the past and plan for the future it doesn't change the present moment.

## 5. Me and You

There are two sides to every coin. There is 'me' and 'you.' This is only one example of why that I think it is so important to be equally passionate about giving as receiving.

## 6. Amazing!

I recently encountered a stranger on the street who stopped and smiled. She then said "you have amazing blue eyes!" Of course it can seem to be an ego boost to get such a nice compliment from a beautiful woman. It was a wonderful compliment, but I didn't really feel or get an ego boost.

It was very clear in that moment that I should acknowledge the compliment and also realize that the ego means nothing. This realization was an amazing revelation so the whole experience made perfect sense.

I smiled and said "thank you" before going on my way.

At that same moment another young lady smiled as she observed this incident. It was an amazing moment. When we pay attention we experience one amazing moment after another.

## 7. WOW!

We can see and experience more amazing things in life when we pay more attention to what's really going on. We have a tendency to believe that the physical images of what we see and experience is what reality is. NOT! Sometimes we like what we see and sometimes we don't. Reality may manifest as things we see and experience, but our existence itself is conscious living whether it can be humanly defined or not. Having said that, every day we can have at least one WOW moment. That experience where we say to ourselves… WOW… that was amazing!

## 8. Modesty

One weekend I went to the beach and worked out with an interesting mix of locals representing the cross section of diversity that lives in Southern California. I found myself in conversation with one young gentleman in particular who was Japanese born and raised. Since I was somewhat familiar with Japanese culture after having been there for a while when I was younger, we talked some about that and particularly the permeating aspect of respect and honor which has been a very important part of Japanese life for centuries.

Though he is now a U.S. citizen and does enjoy living in California, there is also a desire to return to his native country one day and not just for a visit. When I asked why he now wants to do this his reply was something like this:
When first arriving in the U.S., his first impression was that the people here in general were going to be more modest than they actually turned out to be... at least from his perspective.

I could tell that it was a statement that was very heartfelt and not just off the top of his head. He had some time to assimilate some feelings on the subject. There was a part of me that was a little sad, but I could also empathize with him at the same time.

Volumes of material could be written on the subject of modesty. True humility produces true modesty. Some individuals seem to need more of it than others. Modesty may seem to be in short supply sometimes, but it doesn't matter. What really matters is that modesty is essential to what I would call a genuinely high quality of life.

### 9. Passion
What is my passion?

This is a question that many people will hopefully ask themselves as they find themselves either by choice or forced to make major changes in their lives. This is another way of saying *what do I want to do with my life*, or *what is the purpose for being here*, or *what really gets me excited about living*, or *what is my legacy in this world*, or *what is the ultimate goal*, or *what is my dream career*, or *what really makes me feel happy every day?*

Many books are written about this question and how to answer it. My view of this is quite simple. Be aware of living in the present moment every waking moment... or at least do the best you can to pay attention to the moment you are living in and let the revelations or the answers to any questions come to you naturally by not thinking about everything all of the time. Relax your mind by meditating or whatever works to quiet those thoughts that usually are constantly streaming through the mind.

The outcome doesn't have to be anticipated other than it is all right; whatever that is. You are still conscious, right? So don't worry if you have a dilemma and 'just can't seem to figure it out right now.' This is what is interesting about living with this kind of priority and perspective. Being actively present is enough... for NOW.

## 10. The Magic of Life

When I speak of magic I'm not only referring to magicians with card tricks or illusionists with elaborate stage shows.

Whenever in Hollywood, I still sense a sort of magic in the air. Even though some people may ask me what I mean by that, I say it's the vibe of excitement that is still associated with the entertainment industry, for one thing. Because Hollywood is viewed as the global entertainment center and the home of the Academy Awards ©, there will always be a lot of activity that attracts millions of aspiring artists, curious tourists and others every year.

These are surely very interesting and fun things, but I also see magic as much more.

It is that part of life which isn't made up of mundane routines, but is perhaps mystical in nature, and certainly always truly vibrant and intensely alive !

## 11. Illusion

Things are not what they appear to be. Have you heard that before? Illusions aren't real. They may appear to be real, but they are not. That is why many of us like to watch movies and television shows. They are non-fictional or fictional stories with non-fictional and fictional characters. The images are created on video, film, and other formats. It has been produced for our entertainment and education. Sometimes illusions are appealing and sometimes they are revolting. Good or bad, I do not advocate denial of or ignoring illusion, but why dwell on it?

## 12. Teamwork

Office staff
Sports organization
Theatre and show cast
Music group
Classroom project
Production crew
Union
School club
Tour director and assistants
United Nations
Fire Department
City, Local, State, Federal government
Military commander and subordinates
Co-Op
Tribe
Yoga or pilates class
Seminar
Church, temple, and synagogue congregation
Think Tank
Activist group
A Collective of any kind
Animal kingdom
and the rest of
Mother nature

Can you think of other examples?  (Use the space below to answer that
question if you want).

### 13. Food For Thought

A great diet is like a pure thought. When you feel good, your mind should be clear.

### 14. The Consciousness of Teamwork

We are born into this world alone is what we are told. What this means is that each one of us is aware that we are conscious; we are alive and no one else can be conscious for us and we can't be conscious for someone else.

Aside from that, we have to connect, work, and socialize with, and somehow acknowledge others.

This is why teamwork is so important. No one in the so-called human world of day to day living can be without some kind of contact with others unless they just want to live as a hermit in some kind of nomadic experience or something like that.

### 15. Universal Principle

Some philosophical, scientific, religious and other types of analysts evaluate the totality of the Universe in terms of principles. I think a simpler way to discuss principles as complete and not in partial terms would be to say that there is just.... one Universal Principle. It's the same as saying 'we all are one.' Get it?

### 16. A DREAM

A dream is an experience during a sleeping state that for a moment can seem to be real, but actually isn't.

A dream is sometimes associated with a goal of some kind.

A dream may be called a wish for something to come true.

A dream can seem to be an individual experience and it can seem to be a shared experience.

Are dreams real? This can be debated, but I say when we know we are conscious… this is what is actually real; regardless of whether or not you call the experience of this moment a dream.

## 17. SMILE

When I think or say the word 'smile' it makes me smile.

## 18. Happiness

This word *happiness* paints so many pictures when I say it, write it, think about it, etc. There are many perceptions about happiness and most humans put a time element on it. This thing or this person or this experience or this feeling… makes me happy. But the feeling is always the same. It is an unexplainable experience of elation of some kind that usually seems to have a beginning and therefore an end. The NOW moment is Eternal and isn't limited in any way. Happiness should therefore be a constant experience as simple awareness of being; being conscious of consciousness itself. I AM HERE. It really is that simple and that feeling of happiness is immediately recognized when *being conscious* is the only focus of our attention at any moment. How life manifests itself in forms is really fleeting. Don't sweat it if you aren't happy at the moment. This moment passes. Take advantage of that moment passing to realize that happiness is as simple as being conscious….. NOW!

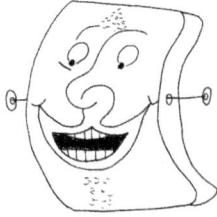

## 19. LAUGHTER

I love to laugh. What about you? There are times when a certain joke or spontaneous experience gets my funny bone or something and I literally laugh out loud and sometimes uncontrollably for a long time!

## 20. EXERCISE (the physical type)

Today I was outdoors exercising in a place in nature, a park that I enjoy visiting. There is a short trail with about fifty cement stairs going down into a ravine in the foothills of the local mountains. The park itself goes through a canyon for miles.

Once upon a time, I almost always used machines to do the work of tackling inclines. It feels so invigorating to utilize what nature has so beautifully created to get a lower body workout; well, except for the cement stairs anyway. I don't by any means suggest the discontinuation of a gym membership, but finding alternatives for the sake of variety to liven up regular routines is always a good thing.

## 21. RENEWAL

Humans have this fascination with birthdates and celebrating birthdays. NOW, I'm not trying to be critical here, but I think celebrating birthdays is overrated. However, celebrating a renewal is
something else. Even cells in the body renew themselves. I think a birthday symbolizing a revitalization of life, even cells in the body is actually a renewal. So I like to say 'Happy Renewal Day' and then….. let's CELEBRATE! What should I do NOW?

## 22. UNIQUE and INTERESTING

The other day while moving about the city incognito (as all of us superheroes must do), a man approached me and told me that I have a very unique and interesting look. I thanked him and smiled and he smiled and walked away.

Each one of us actually is unique and interesting. This could be your moment to realize that as you are reading this.

## 23. WE ARE NOT ALONE

We are not alone in the Universe. This sounds like a statement out of a science fiction novel or movie trailer. In fact, it would most likely be more accurate to say that we aren't lonely. Being alone is not such a bad thing really. Sometimes we need that private quiet time to just contemplate the moment where we are.

Extraterrestrials, or whoever or whatever must be *out there* in the Universe (get real we don't know what they call themselves). It's doubtful that they would call themselves aliens, extraterrestrials, little green men, alien grays, space cadets, etc. The fact that millions of people on planet Earth will say that they feel we can't be alone in the Universe, should be proof enough that we are in fact not alone.

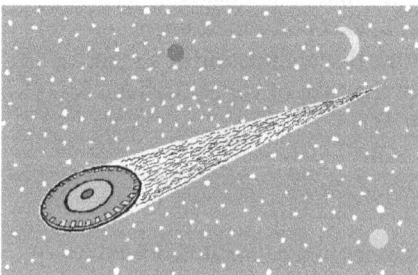

## 24. INNOVATION

is such an interesting word. When I use this word I think of ideas, concepts, products, and ways of doing things that are totally original and continually fresh. We need more innovation not less. I think we should also build onto the innovations that have been fruitful and truly productive for this planet that we call home which includes the totality of its' diversity of inhabitants. I'm not just writing words that you are reading in this moment, there are necessary actions for all of us to embrace NOW!

What actions am I talking about?
Check out *Exercise (the Spiritual type)* to help answer that question.

## 25. Exercise (the Spiritual type)

1. Come up with a goal
2. Prepare a plan
3. Create at least one kind of activity everyday that is essential to the plan and the eventual completion of the goal
4. Write a mantra for each part of the plan
5. Repeat the mantras daily and with each day increase the number of times that you repeat them
6. As you continue the first five steps of this exercise, start paying attention to how activities and then goals in life are unfolding... look for productive patterns that duplicate and take notes if you need to
7. Repeat this exercise every time that you come up with a goal

## 26.  EVERYONE IN THIS PLACE MAKES THE WORLD GO AROUND

Each individual is conscious, or in other words, is aware of being here and NOW therefore each one of us is Consciousness.  Anything else perceived is an illusion really.  Of course each individual must recognize that we are all actually one Consciousness in the Eternal NOW!  Everyone together is essential to the existence of the Universe… that is what I mean when I say everyone makes the world go around.

After all, what else could it actually be?  Is there really chaos in the Universe, or did we just imagine that to be the case? These are just some ideas to consider and thoughts to contemplate…

## 27. THE BEAUTY OF ART

Today I attended a bi-annual event at an old brewery in downtown Los Angeles that is an open house event for a multitude of artists living and working in lofts.

It was truly an inspiring experience with a vast array of artistic styles from painting to sculpture, from cloth to canvas and steel to clay, from furniture and prop building to costume and jewelry and even the design of gourmet food, from one to two dimensional, from cardboard 3D glasses to make shift view master projectors, from realist to abstract, from photography to drawing... you get the idea. Of course artists are usually eccentric fun loving types of people who are adamant about the connection of themselves and their art with an audience. The intimacy of the lofts where the artists themselves often call home is as beautiful of an experience as the transcendent art forms themselves.

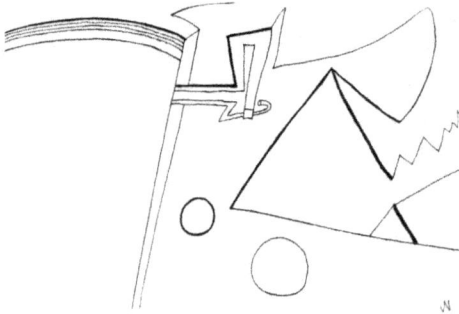

## 28. NO FEAR

What real purpose could fear actually serve? Perhaps the purpose could be stated as a way to show us that there really isn't anything to fear.

## 29. NO CHANGE

The NOW moment doesn't really change because the moment is always NOW. You might question that statement, but when I talk about the NOW moment I'm not talking about *the illusion that is called the now moment*. The illusion seems to be a lot of things which are contrary to what the NOW moment is. It kind of sounds like a mantra to say that **there is no change**, but in the Eternal NOW there really isn't anything that changes.

## 30. DOO DAH, DOO DAH

Doo Dah is a term that I know of which comes from the lyrics of a song called 'Camptown Races' and it is also the name of a famous silly annual parade of street performers that I have appeared in. It takes place every year in Pasadena, California.

Sometimes humans just take themselves so seriously. My suggestion is to never take oneself too seriously. Even though we take our work seriously and we should be responsible of course, we should still also take a moment here and there to just enjoy being present in the present moment.

## 31. MONEY

What is money anyway? How important is money really especially when it has no value? That has happened throughout history, you know! There was the Continental here in U.S. history and the Zim (Zimbabwe) dollar in the 21$^{st}$ century, for instance.

You can be happy with it, you can be happy without it. You can be miserable with it or without it. Money doesn't create happiness, ok, so we know that is true. We also can say we have come to the conclusion that it 'can seem' to add to one's already existing happiness somehow or at least pay bills.

Money actually doesn't create anything of course. In personal relationships it is often the reason given for rifts between people due to over-exaggerated emphasis and importance that only humans place upon it. Some people are so attached to it, that they carry body language around with an air of superiority and arrogance that to me looks more like varying degrees of personal insecurity.

Is money the root of all evil? It would be more accurate to say the attitude behind it determines the outcome of any circumstance… not the actual money itself. Have you looked at money? It is like artwork that has been handled by who knows how many people. Coins are actually two dimensional. All currency has two sides to it, too.

It is best NOW, as I understand, to realize just what money is and to not use it to determine the circumstances of every part of life especially relationships with other human beings, animals, and other forms of life on this planet. You really 'can't take it with you' which is another old expression I am referencing here. If you allow it to control your life in determining your relationships and every aspect of your life experience, you are the one who is missing the point.

NOW is the present moment to enjoy and LIVE regardless of the amount of money in your bank account or your wallet and the same can be said of your investment accounts and even your mattresses… in the event you've started stashing your money there.

*Question*: Do you think we will ever get to a point where we won't really need money anymore?

**NOWMAN:** I think we have to get to the point where there isn't greed first, but we will probably still have the currency of the present moment.

**32. A NOW Joke:**
(Mother's Day)

Question: What could you call a gift to your mother on *Mother's Day*?

Answer: The Present MOMent.

**33. NOWsense:  Global Warming**

There is some kind of global warming…. in the hearts of many people on our planet. That is the kind of global warming that makes sense.

Cold hearts let alone closed minds in human beings cannot be a good thing.

## 34. What do you want to be when you grow up?

This is a phrase that really makes no sense. I know that it usually refers to the individual's life goal or goals especially when it comes to career direction.

What is growing up?
 Is it maturity?
Is it considered getting older in physical years or emotional feelings?

This thought or some other similar thought seems to pop into your head. You then find yourself saying it out loud or hear others say it and automatically assume that you know what it means, but do you know what it means?

The present moment is what is actually important here.
Stay focused on that and try not to think in terms of some future event called 'growing up.' Staying focused on the present should even help you answer the question with clarity and little or no stress.

## 35. Do you get it?

Do you get it? Has someone ever said this to you? Have you ever heard someone ask another person that question?

Everyone would probably like to think that they do get it or in other words.... aren't clueless.

What am I talking about? Maybe I am referring to the basic subject of life itself. What is life? Do I get it? Do you get it? Do you and I understand 'it' and just what is 'it?'
Everything existing in this moment is consciousness, and we are conscious...so do we 'get it' right NOW? Do we understand that understanding this concept should be right in front of our faces, so-to-speak.... right NOW?

I hope you aren't confused. This should all be simple to explain, but it is amazing how complex it can seem to be at the same time. The Universe is a vast unexplainable thing or some kind of thing. I think that it's ok to leave it at that.

I do want to elaborate more on this expression centered around 'getting it.' There is another expression that goes something like this: Life is just a dream.

Billions of people are walking around like they are in a dream; most are walking around like they are sound asleep or half awake, and very few seem to be walking in the dream fully awake.

**BLOG Excerpts # 1:**

36. NOWism 1–
I hear a lot of talk about HOPE and CHANGE. How can I hope for a future that doesn't exist? I do have some coins in my pocket though.

37. NOWism 2–
Question– Why is it that *some guys get all the luck*, you know like the lyrics of that popular song? NOWMAN: That song also says some guys do nothing but complain. Luck can change, but the moment is always NOW. It isn't luck that makes a moment exist.

38. NOWism 3–
Living NOW means paying attention NOW! What is an example of paying attention? If you believe you must dwell on the past or the future.. that isn't the present moment so.... Be Here NOW!

39. NOWism 4– Einstein would probably say something like time is relative, but I say NOW is all that IS!

40. NOWism 5– Treat others like you want to be treated is a great philosophy of every moment!

41. NOWism 6– The present moment is actually unavoidable, but attention to it is required in order to understand that.

42. NOWism 7 – The ego isn't real because it is only a temporary appearance. The NOW moment is constant Reality!

43. NOWism 8– The ego is a distraction of the mind from paying attention to the present moment.

44. NOWism– 9
The past is pointless unless a lesson is applicable NOW... just like the future is pointless unless a journey and destination is necessary for a plan that is being created NOW.

45. NOWism– 10
NOW isn't a state of mind, it IS the present moment. It is so easy to start dwelling on the past and the future. Keep it simple for your sanity, All that exists is NOW!

46. NOWism– 11
What are you focusing on right NOW? Even when you think about the past and future, you are thinking about it NOW.

47. NOWism– 12
How do we live in the moment? Pay attention to what is happening consciously first as an observer and when you must act, do not take the human experience too seriously. At the same time however, there is Principle and order in the Universe.

48. NOWism– 13
Are you paying attention to being present in the present moment each moment?

49. NOWism– 14
The moment is always NOW so that simplifies the decision about 'what to do' NOW.

50. NOWism– 15
The present moment is undeniable when paying attention. The illusion of this human experience is likewise undeniable because for some reason humans are meant to experience it, right ?

## 51. NOWism– 16

Relax. We are each conscious that we are conscious NOW. It may not look that way sometimes, but we are conscious. If you're reading this you're conscious!

## 52. NOWism– 17
At Farmer's Market NOW.... Living in the moment is like the produce... always fresh!

## 53. NOWism– 18
Waking up in the morning (or whenever your normal waking up time is) is a great example of a great moment to be fully conscious of the present moment. It's a great way to start the day!

## 54. NOWism– 19
I hope that when you read this you are fully conscious of being in the moment and if you aren't really feeling it... just be patient you will if you truly desire to.. Actually, we never really leave the moment, it only seems like there are distractions.

## 55. NOWism– 20
Sometimes life seems so full of details that it is better than watching a movie. Other times life seems ordinary and maybe even a bit bland if you try to compare it to other things in life. It's all amazing because we are aware that we exist each and every moment when we pay attention. Stay present with awareness and you'll see how profound life is regardless of the appearances.

## 56. NOWism– 21

You are reading this NOW, so you know that it is possible to be aware of paying attention to the moment NOW.. Feel the feeling just knowing that this moment exists and when you pay attention, it naturally reduces some anxiety. Be Here Now......

57. NOWism– 22

Are you anxious about the future and have regrets from the past? Well, you know what I have to say to that! NOW is all that is real ! The Universe is complex but the Universal Law of the Eternal and Infinite NOW is quite clear and simple. Be Here Now.....

## 58. WRITER'S BLOCK

The flow of life can never actually be blocked and you don't have to be a writer to know the feeling of seeming out of sync or possibly lacking motivation.   Here NOW it is impossible to be out of sync because the present moment is always complete and what happens naturally is always free flowing. How can that in itself not be inspiring?

If it seems like you should do something else or you feel stuck in a given moment that may seem to repeat itself over and over again... then at least try to do something else... NOW!

## 59. THE GOLDEN RULE

Treat others like you want to be treated.  That is certainly not an original idea, but it is an Eternal Fact and Universal Law.  I think it is a great idea to contemplate the meaning.... NOW!

**BLOG excerpts # 2:**

60. NOWism– 23

Debt crisis or any kind of crisis implies lack. I am not suggesting that we deny the deep problems caused by some humans and their egos.  Quite the contrary, we must be constantly alert and deliberately dispel all illusions!

We can believe whatever we want about the Universe, but the Universe is full of Abundance and the NOW moment is not only the primary concern, but all that actually exists in Reality. Pay attention!

**61**. NOWism– 24

When we fall asleep, (for most humans, this happens at night after the sun sets), we do at some point wake up to start a new day. So... waking up isn't an option, really... is it?

## 62. THE OCEAN

I love the beach and when I look out to the horizon and cannot see the end of a water line with the human eyes, it is truly inspiring. It is one of the ways that I sense the Infinity of Life in the present moment.

## 63. BUSINESS

We often forget that business is just another way of saying busy-ness. We are constantly busy. The human body is constantly moving even when we are sleeping and appear to be sitting still. The blood is constantly circulating through the veins. The cells and the digestive track are always in motion, for instance.

The earth is constantly moving... turning and revolving around the sun even though we only see the sun rising and setting within 24 hours. In a nutshell, we are all busy whether we want to be or not and things are not what they appear to be.. NOW and forever!

**64.** *Question:*
What does it mean when you say 'ETERNAL NOW?'
**NOWMAN:**
That is a good question. It could be answered in unlimited ways because it is impossible to put a limitation on the meaning of timeless presence in the present moment. Does it sound like I'm intellectualizing? It is impossible to be too simple with this. It does suffice 'to say' all that exists is right now, this very moment, etc., but living this talk isn't as simple as it may seem. It's like practicing a musical instrument or maintaining a talent or skill, we just keep moving... We really don't have a choice about NOW... we just have to pay attention so that we better understand the ETERNAL aspect of the Universe that is the NOW.

## 65. ILLUSION OF DUALITY

The human experience seems to be full of duality ... good and bad, hot and cold, open and closed, love and hate, night and day, dark and light, left and right, liberal and conservative, physical temporal and the Spiritual Eternal, binary (1 and 2), etc. The appearance of duality is strange because when contemplating the Universe, could there really be two or more universes or two or more of ALL? I mean, isn't the Universe Itself just like the present moment NOW... ALL that exists?

What am I talking about?

For instance, have you heard this common expression used by peace activists, musicians, or new age practitioners?....
*"WE ALL ARE ONE."*

That's one, not two or more. We don't say 'we all are two.' ONE Universe, ONE NOW moment this very moment is our whole existence.

**66. Question: What is the meaning of life?**

**NOWMAN:** First of all what do you mean by life? If you are referring to human life which actually is not at all what it seems, then that definition would be very limited. If by LIFE you mean the Universe, then life is truly Eternal which by definition means without beginning and without ending and Infinite which means no limitations. That must mean Intelligence and Perfection manifests Itself when that is the case, right? Contemplate that one for a while!

**67. PEACE (NOT WAR)**

Many poems, stories and songs have been written on the subject of peace as a direct reaction to war. How could anyone promote the opposite of peace especially for the purpose of personal economic gain at the expense of other human, also animal and all life forms? It is time to wake up NOW! There are no delays or future requirements in order to wake up NOW. Peace is NOW!

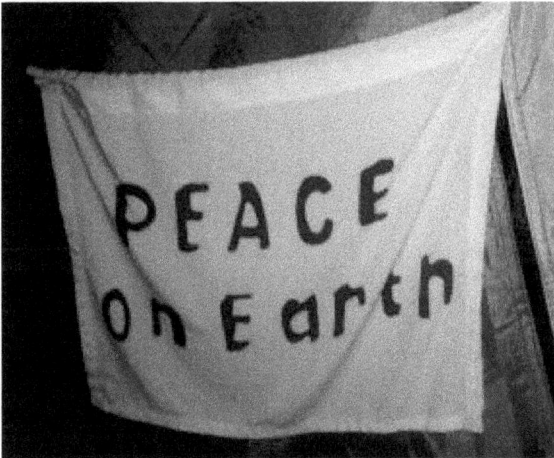

## 68. SPRING IN TO ACTION !

The first day of spring comes in late March and signals the beginning of warmer weather for some people in the western hemisphere. For some it is the time of the year when nature blossoms in so many ways with beautiful flowers and small gardens, and farmers plant their seeds in many acres of farmland in order to get the process started for the vast majority of the agricultural production of the year.

For some, it is school graduation and a new start of some kind during the 'coming of age' process in one's own little world so-to-speak. It could be the start of a new job or career. It could be an activist cause that you are passionate about.

Regardless of your beliefs, it definitely alludes to the idea that a forward motion is happening. Roll with it. It is a stream of consciousness, but definitely make thoughtful clarity the primary motivation.

## 69. STREAM OF CONSCIOUSNESS

Prolific writers often experience moments when they just start writing like I'm actually doing right NOW in what could be called a 'stream of consciousness.' This basically means one just gets into a flow in this case writing and in my case typing on a computer and whatever comes out is spontaneous and definitively in the moment! Sometimes when going back to look at what was written, the writer may say, ewww, where did that come from? It is time for serious revision or even start over already. Then there are those other times like magic where the writer may ask himself or herself, WOW that is amazing! What just happened here?

It didn't come from anywhere really. It is after all a constant stream of inspiration just manifesting as quickly as it can be written down. The meaning can be interpreted later. I am enjoying this MOMENT as I am typing because I have no expectation of what I am going to write next or how long this segment will be. It is truly a magnificent feeling as I can sense the stream of consciousness 'clearly' unfolding before my own eyes.

So NOW I feel like I need to make some kind of point here perhaps as a closing statement of some kind. I don't want to sound like I am about to say something predictably profound and then you read this with the expectation that I am about to say something profound. The words affect us in different ways and that is what can be interesting about this whole experience.

Are you feeling very clearly at this moment that you are conscious this very moment? Is NOW at the forefront of your mind and experience? Yes? Great, then you have paid attention. Keep doing that and even more amazing things will reveal themselves. It is totally natural to keep the attention focused on the Here and NOW!

## 70. MORE ON DUALITY

Not to dwell on it, but if one has a question about duality I think we must first look at the human life, the human situation, the human condition, anything... human.

It is an appearance of consciousness in form, but it is just an appearance. We should neither dwell on nor deny the appearances of things. Consciousness is real substance in form, but it isn't what it appears to be. Likewise this human experience or appearance or illusion is not what it appears to be, but we are experiencing this for some purpose.

I like to distinguish between Reality and an illusion. Illusion seems to validate the 'apparent' duality of the human experience.

Take the words (and the meanings) of the words LOVE and hate. Both are attitudes that human beings can seem to possess. Hate would be an illusive attitude because LOVE is that intangible tangible which seems to connect us with the Soul, the Universe, and the Eternal. When LOVE is the focus, hate just seems to fade away in importance and attention because LOVE is the actual Reality.

**BLOG Excerpts # 3**

**71.** NOWism 25-

That which is truly the most important in life is the most important for a purpose. Everything else just isn't as important.

**72.** NOWism 26-

If the future seems to happen fast, that is, 'it seems to be here before you know it,' like the expression goes, then NOW is even faster and it happens every moment.

**73. The Compassion of Responsibility and the Responsibility of Compassion**

Compassion is necessary whether we choose to show it to others or also to ourselves. Each one of us is an individual being and soul.

The words *personal responsibility* may refer to what we as individuals can do to contribute to society somehow in a positive fashion, but when I say the compassion of responsibility, it is also an attitude of compassion shown to those around us and to others around the world when that is truly our focus.

Charity is not always the correct word here. Giving should be a regular behavior and not always viewed as charity but as a way of life especially when we are immersed in abundance of one kind or many kinds.

The responsibility of compassion, is the necessity of being compassionate as we live our lives. It is a way of life always wherever we are along the path in this journey.

## 74. FAMILY

The family is another word for connection and is usually associated with human connections. It doesn't necessarily mean exclusively a biological family. Most humans don't really seem to understand that the biological is just one aspect of family. There are some lighter views concerning the meaning of family. For instance, there is the term 'extended family' which is a loose term that may include old friends and in-laws' families perhaps, but there is still this illusive belief that it really isn't the core family.

It is so easy to limit one's concept of what the family is solely because of human constraints such as the biology, time (how long you've known someone or focusing on the so-called limited number of hours in the day which is often used as an excuse for not making a deeper connection- you know that statement: "I just don't have the time," but we know fully well that we make the time for what we really want to make the time for), old habits and traditions, and whatever else can arise.

Sometimes laziness and personal issues in the relationship can keep someone from contacting another even if they are biologically related. Attachment doesn't mean that you are connected and that this is automatically a family connection, just like detachment doesn't mean disconnection with no family connection whatsoever. I think the key is what is in the heart and you will know to reach out. The flip side of that is you will know when you should let go and let someone else reach out to you. It is more real that way as long as there isn't extreme co-dependence.

Being connected DOESN'T mean extreme co-dependence and though this extreme should be avoided, it often isn't because many people think that extreme co-dependence is normal and if this isn't the action taken then the connection is lost or is very volatile at the very least. Make no mistake, that is an illusion, for sure! Our relationship connections obviously exist for a reason, but sometimes we do get carried away with attachments in human relationships or the opposite when just brushing off emotions, so-to-speak.

There is A LOT that can be written about this subject and I may be inclined to write more about it later.

The family is a Universal connection that is Eternal and isn't limited to biological family, old traditions, extreme co-dependence and absence of independence. It is all-inclusive and pays attention to needs and the purpose of specific connections. This is not to say that we disregard the biological connections. There is a purpose for all connections in the so-called human experience. The key is really to pay attention to the purpose in order to get passed the illusions and live life to the fullest with our ENTIRE FAMILY. The entire family is the UNIVERSAL FAMILY here and NOW!

## 75. SUPPLY

The Universe is Infinite and the human experience which is limited isn't what it appears to be, so it only 'seems' like the supply is running out, limited, dwindling, or even non-existent.
Since Life is Infinite and is the Universe Itself, it is impossible for the supply to run out when the Infinite Universe is the supply Itself.

Now, I am not denying the human experience and all of it's problems, misconceptions, deliberate deceptions and whatever some humans can sometimes seem to create in order to distract us from basic and profound truths about ourselves and the world we live in. Part of not denying this, is to face the illusion head on and then embrace those parts of every conscious experience which serve as our connection to something which is truly Reality.

## 76. MARGINALIZING

It is impossible to marginalize the NOW moment because just like the Universe Itself... it is literally impossible to actually put any kind of limitation or line of demarcation on or around something that is REAL, Infinite and Eternal.

## 77. FEELING SORRY FOR YOURSELF?

Are you feeling sorry for yourself? There are distinctions to make sometimes.

Negativity makes me look toward the positive.

Anger reminds me to chill out and put on a smiling face.

Ignorance wakes me up from my complacent nap.

Selfishness advises that it is better to give.

Self-absorption shows me how silly and limiting that is to think that the world evolves around me.

Get over it.... NOW!

## 78. POSSESSIONS

A friend was having a discussion on social media about seeing possessions left lying around a house by family after a loved one had passed away. He was having an epiphany about the fleetingness of life and the over-emphasis on 'things.'

If looking around your house at all of your stuff seems overwhelming or you feel sad or stressed about downsizing, it isn't that big of a deal, so deal with it. On the other hand, how we treat others and the quality of life in quality time with others IS a big deal!

You don't have to wait for these basic profound realizations. At that moment you are aware... be a good steward, but realize what is most important. Possessions are not top priority and never have been! They're over-rated, too. Embrace it and accept it! NOW!

## 79. What is Love?

I know this question is asked over and over again, but I think that there can never be too much Love in the Universe, do you? First of all, Love is Infinite and Eternal, so there is no shortage of it when we genuinely seek it. Everything happens for a reason and Love is always present. It's obvious when you pay attention to It.

## 80. READ A BOOK DAY

I didn't know until this year that there is actually a Holiday called 'National Read A Book Day.' So…. You're reading a book right NOW! Soooo, wherever you are… join the celebration!

## 81. BALANCE

The world seems to be full of extremes that are just illusions of the human mind, in other words, they aren't real, but it sure seems like it when observing the crazy human world that we call home.

No matter the appearance, how normal or how strange something seems, the illusion never really affects the pure Consciousness of what is REAL and existing as the present moment.

Truth is not an extreme and neither is balance one-sided. Balance is the happy median, medium, the middle, the center, etc.

Balance can be found in any part of the Universe, it always exists, and we just have to pay attention.

**BLOG Excerpt # 4**

82. NOWism 27-

NOW is the moment that you are aware of this moment.

## 83. MEMORY

Is there really a memory? If there actually is such 'a thing' there would have to be a past existence of some kind that a memory would have to remember.

At this point in the so-called human evolution (or whatever you want to call the human experience) a computer or computer stick or flash drive saves information and that information is called memory and the space that it occupies in a drive is called memory space. When the human brain remembers something, anything from the five human senses, it is just called memory.

The present moment doesn't need a memory because there is no past. You could question that and say there was a past when there were many different present moments previous to the one we are currently experiencing, and if you wanted to remember those preceding moments, you would have to have a memory in order to do that. Well, it certainly seems that way.

The human mind rambles on and on about a lot of stuff sometimes, but is that mind real or just the imagination of an illusive mind and all of its' distractions?  At the very least it is some food for thought or something like that.

One thing feels certain to me... focusing on the NOW, the present moment, does make living a lot simpler sometimes. Take a deep breath or two, and just consider the idea of the present moment.  One doesn't need memory to just be aware of the present. It is relaxing and sheds some light on the meaning of life with a unique perspective.

## 84.  FATHER

The father represents the half of human life that is usually referred to as the man, the masculine aspect of humanity, the head of the household, the male gender, the parent, a role model... you get my drift.

When we are kids, a good father figure will often use the word NOW.

Do your homework NOW.
Go to school NOW.
Mow the lawn NOW.
Help your mother NOW.
Respect your elders NOW.
Dinner is ready NOW.
NOW means NOW, not an hour from NOW.
Go get a job NOW.
Shut your mouth NOW.

## 85.  FREEDOM

You are free to believe whatever you want to believe, but it is still a belief.  The most important thing is that you can recognize that you're free to choose what you want to believe or not believe.   Consciousness is free to think about whatever it wants to focus on.  No person or thing can stop you from doing that.  You are free to listen and believe what you are told, or to just choose your own path.

## 86. LABOR?

Humans work and play. Work isn't necessarily work and sometimes play is work. Any activity is much more relevant when it is enjoyable whether we call it work or play. It is interesting that there is a Holiday called Labor Day and it is supposed to be the day that we honor the working people. It should be called No Labor Day, but some people don't get the day off, so for them No Labor Day wouldn't apply. I say whatever you do NOW... enjoy it and work becomes more like play.

## 87. Loyalty

is one of those emotional things in human relationships that seems to have all sorts of conditions to it including a time element attached to it, such as the length of time that the relationship has existed.

Some people celebrate those anniversary dates... such as birthdays and even the date that they met their significant other let alone the wedding date. Not that there is anything wrong with that.

The NOW is also about having FUN and enjoying the company of those around us. When our attention is on 'being present in the NOW,' that is all we are really aware of.

How about showing some loyalty and love by giving someone a hug right NOW!

## 88. UNIQUENESS and ORIGINALITY

I have already written about unique and interesting which are two of my favorite words (probably two out of a million words that I could say are my favorites..lol). I also want to put uniqueness and originality together as well and elaborate a little bit on that combination and why I think it is good to mention it.

Many people associate originality with the artist (original music, original art, original idea, etc.), but just being an original artist doesn't necessarily mean that you automatically recognize your uniqueness as well. So you ask, what do I mean by that?

There are countless examples of original thinking just like original art expressions. There are many original pieces of art that 'remind' you of some other artist for instance, but you can't really define it as uniquely original. It is one thing to be inspired by an artist and another to analyze and semi-copy that artist in some way. When you know that you think, act and live outside the box, so-to-speak and /or really know that you are doing something or a combination of things that literally hasn't been done before, then you know that you are at least beginning to understand and recognize that you are unique. It is not so easy to describe that in words and I hope to be better at it, the more that I write about it and hopefully and humbly understand it.

I try to express feelings in this written form. It is like trying to describe the concept of living in the present moment as I do in this book over and over in various ways. It is like a stream of consciousness that flows as I type these words.

As we all go about our daily lives whether we pay attention to that natural flow or not, we really do recognize our uniqueness each moment. That recognition is also the same so-called feeling of conscious being, being aware of the constant presence that you (and I and everyone and everything) are alive and we exist, for instance. This awareness is what manifests the understanding of the greatness of all things unique AND original.

*Question:* What did you just say?  Come down to Earth would you please NOWMAN.

NOWMAN:  OK, Here is the simplest way of putting it:

Pay attention to the UNIQUENESS that you are... NOW!

### 89. Communication

Human beings often find themselves in situations where there is miscommunication.  Details can be very complex you know and that explains why there seems to be so much misunderstanding. It's like trying to analyze the Universe in one sentence. There are probably an infinitude of ways to do that, and I think we all do it every day, but along with the words we must understand the meaning of those words especially used in combination.  This is where communication comes into our lives.

Some people seem to be better at this than others, but we always feel better when we learn to communicate more clearly, more thoroughly, and more honestly.  I mean, we feel better in every way, mentally, emotionally, and even physically and Spiritually.  There could be more to that as well, but I wanted to make the point that there are many benefits to being GREAT COMMUNICATORS.

I'm not talking about just being good at selling something. It depends on 'how' you go about selling 'what' you are selling.  Being NOWMAN, obviously I am not trying to sell you on the idea of the present moment, but I am at least attempting to communicate that awareness that I see as my mission.  You can take it or leave it, I am just BEING present and you are, too.

What would you like to communicate with me?  I'm all ears.  Well, you know what I mean.

## 90. Music

is one of those tangible non-tangible things that somehow magically seems to connect us to what seems to be (the invisible) reality that we somehow know consciously is what is really going on as we live our day- to- day lives. It is analyzed as things such as notes, melodies, rhythms, sounds, compositions, instruments, recordings, groups, solo artists, live concerts, and so many unique and distinctive styles, writers, and players.

It really is amazing how it just gets to the heart, the soul, the adrenaline, the passions, and a plethora of outward emotions and expressions.

Perhaps the greatest thing about it is that we can just simply enjoy listening and are magically transformed or transported.

What are you listening to NOW?

## 91. LISTENING

What are listening to right NOW?  Do you hear birds singing?  Do you hear the white noise of a fan or outside traffic?  Do you hear an expresso coffee machine or a juicer machine?  Do you hear voices talking around you?  Do you hear a dog barking? Do you hear someone singing or playing an instrument?

Do you hear silence?

## 92. ADVENTURES of NOWMAN

Did you have at least one adventure today? Each moment is actually an adventure in some way or another. Consider that for a moment.

## 93. CAREER SEMINAR IN A MOMENT
Make a list with each following question.

*What are your passions?*

*What is your work experience and education or training?*

*What are your own special skills and talents?*

*What are the needs in the community and the world?*

NOW, after have you completed these questions. Share them with friends and family whose views that you respect and see what their feedback is.

On your own, contemplate how all four areas are connected and then you can clearly start researching possibilities.

## 94. CONTEMPLATION 1

Consider the moment… wherever you seem to be right NOW.

What is really important?

Did you get some food for the Soul as well as the belly?

Do you have a roof over your head? During the daytime, look up to the sky at some point.

Do you have enough clothing to wear on your physical body? Are you open or have you covered your Soul?

Open up.

Consider this.

## 95.  CONTEMPLATION 2:

Consider the moment… whatever you are doing right NOW.

What are thinking about?

Are you focused on what you are doing right now or are you distracted?

If you are distracted, you must have wanted to be distracted.

Let even the word *contemplation* be like a mantra to repeat.

## 96.  CONTEMPLATION 3:

Consider the moment… who are you?

What is your identity anyway?

Consider the Consciousness that you are aware of being regardless of what human forms and thoughts seem to be around you…even your own.

Just let your thoughts go so that the needless meandering stops and you are just aware of being present this moment.

Enjoy the presence of just being…… NOW!

## 97.  NO TIME, NO SPACE

Consciousness can't really be measured and doesn't really fit into any time and space continuum.  It doesn't start and stop, fluctuate, come and go, exist sooner or later, etc.  There is no appearance of time and space other than in the illusive human experience. I know that sounds a bit out there, but Consciousness is awareness that isn't limited by beginning and ending and the birth and death of anything either.

Consider this.

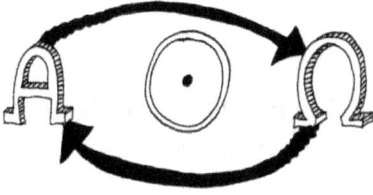

Alpha and Omega

## 98. DAY AND NIGHT

*Question*:  You say that there is no time or space and all that exists is NOW, but how do you account for the changing of day into night into day, the sunset and sunrise, etc. It looks like time passing.

**NOWMAN**: I don't account for it. I don't deny it. It is 'how' we look at it that is important. We seem to be living this human experience for some specific reason or for specific reasons. It really isn't that big of a deal other than the fact that we are here to live through whatever this life leads us into.  That is all.

NOW, day and night, sunrises and sunsets all appear to prove the passing of time, but that is really all to be said about it. Just enjoy the beauty of that great sunrise or sunset and live the present moment.  When that passes, live that moment. When that moment passes, live the next moment and so on.

## 99. SPOOKY

Do you believe in ghosts? They are often the subjects of books, films, plays or conversations amongst interesting people.

Sometimes ghosts are called spirits and sometimes they are said to be haunting or spooky, but they look harmless to me. I often will say *'things are not what they appear to be'* and that is so true, as I see it.

What is your perception? Have you been taught to think of spooky as something that is un-natural and perhaps something demonic? I hope that isn't the case.

Does spooky mean that someone or something can be 'ghost-like?'

Spooky has a whole other meaning when you put it in the context of learning a lesson of some kind.

In the present moment, we are to enjoy this human experience as much as possible and to at least begin to indulge ourselves in non-denial. Once we understand something isn't real and as long as it is sanely appealing, we can just have fun with it.

## 100. Eternal Lasts Forever

You know the phrase 'nothing lasts forever?' That is true when we are discussing the so-called human condition. The timeless and endless Eternal NOW, as I like to call it, is forever because that is exactly what the word eternal means. There really isn't measurable time even though it may seem like there is.

There are other words in the English language that conjure up pictures of something more permanent such as: veteran, tenure and endurance, for instance.

No matter how we look at it, illusion isn't real so everything REAL is Eternal and NOW

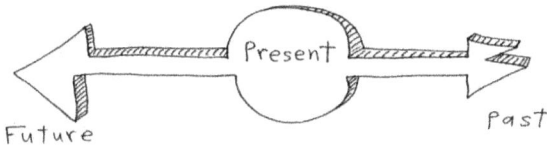

Future — Present — Past

## 101. What is REAL?
*Question:* What is REAL?
**NOWMAN:** REAL is that which is timeless and spaceless, Infinite and Eternal and that is in the context of the present moment. It is like a feeling to be experienced or something like that. It's like the light bulb going off throughout your entire being. It really is impossible to pin it down to one human explanation because it isn't really a human experience.

**102. HUMANS AND THE HUMAN EXPERIENCE AREN'T PERFECTION, BUT......**have you ever had an experience that made you realize that you had experienced something other-worldly, more than coincidental, orderly but not typical, and otherwise humanly indescribable? That is Perfection manifesting itself through what would ordinarily seem imperfect. Once we start to see this somehow it is as if we are transformed and look at life and the Universe in a much different way!

A pattern of these experiences hopefully will begin. It is the already existing Perfection starting to get through consciously and as we are open, we seem to experience it more and more. Actually, Perfection is constant. Stay alert!

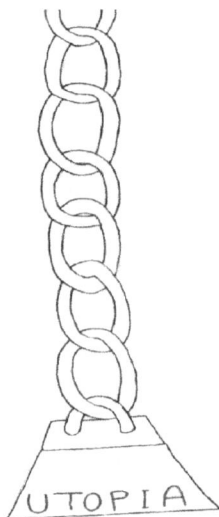

## 103. CLOCKS

have long served the purpose of telling us the time of day or night.  It seems like as our gadgets for telling the time become more 'so-called' sophisticated, we start looking more and more at where the sun is in the sky.

Even the 'biological' clock, as I often hear the females of the species often mention, means some sort of inner awareness is taking place.  Maybe males can feel this, too, sometimes.

Maybe we individually and collectively are clearly recognizing the timelessness of the Eternal
NOW!

The {NOW} watch

## 104. CHEESY

Do you like cheese? I feel a bit silly at the moment. Let's see, when I think of cheese I think of:
 A plethora of certain dairy products from all around the world
Cows mooing
A chip dip
A type of organ keyboard sound
A style of music
A certain kind of joke
A delicious sandwich
The stomach growling at the moment

Add your own:

## 105. The Internet

Is the Internet a symbol of the Eternal? Discuss this if you'd like.

## 106. KINDNESS

is mandatory in my life. What about you?
It ties in with the need to show and to be shown compassion.

## 107. SENSES

Are there five human senses? Some say that there is an intuitive sixth sense. Some say more perhaps even an infinity of senses.

I say there is just one... The Consciousness that is the Present Moment.

## 108.  RAINBOW

When I see a rainbow in the sky, and I have seen and flown through some incredible rainbows. They are so beautiful, I have to stop and stare.

Even though aware of an array of different colors, I really just focus on the beauty of the one multi-colored experience and what the symbol actually stands for.

We really all are ONE Consciousness, ONE Presence, and ONE BEING... experiencing something that is more than just what appears.

Contemplate that NOW.

## 109.  MOMENTUM

Are you on a roll?  Sometimes I am, I tell you.

When the Present Moment is the only real focus of attention, you can't possibly disrupt, stop, and restart momentum.

## 110.  BACKWARDS and FORWARDS

In the present moment, here NOW, we realize that no one is actually going anywhere in some space and time continuum.  It might seem like it sometimes, but sometimes just the use of words can assist us with focus and sometimes they can distract, so that is why paying attention is so important.

If it seems like you have to take a step back just to take a step forward, don't sweat it.  You're still living in the Present Moment and aren't really bound by time.  That being said, why wait for some future enlightenment?

## 111.  SAME MEANING

The glass that is half full is the same as the glass that is half empty.  Six is the same as a half a dozen.  The season autumn is also called fall.  The Present Moment is NOW!

## 112. QUIET

I'm sitting in a quiet room being quiet at the moment. Sometimes the best place in our day-to-day busy lives is to sit alone in a quiet room, or in a quiet room with others if that is possible. It isn't mandatory though, if you want to quiet down your busy thoughts. I have had some very quiet moments walking down streets of some of the most humanly populated cities in the world. It really is 'how' you listen to the inner voice that is most important.

## 113. FORGIVENESS
SOUL
is such an important word for our dialogue because it really does mean *'for the purpose of giving and the act of giving.'* When an error is made, by ourselves or someone else, the act of forgiveness seems to relieve a huge burden of some kind. It really is indescribable. It can be realized and expressed in the same moment.

## 114. WORDS

Here is a list of words that are good to frequently visit in the repertory of your mind and heart:
Love
Contemplation
Present Moment
NOW
Consciousness
Peace
Awareness

FUN
(Don't always take yourself too seriously)

## 115. EVERYTHING

Infinity includes ALL that is REAL. Everything that is REAL actually exists Eternally. Eternity is NOW because the present moment is the Eternal NOW!

## 116. PICTURES

Pictures are things we look at. Appearances, including what we look at in a picture, are not what they appear to be.

## 117. SOUL

Soul is often considered the human connection to the Spiritual. It is invisible to the human in daily life because humans are so accustomed to the appearances of physical objects. It is often believed to be that part of life that is eternal.

## 118. COMMON SENSE

If making sense is really a common thing, wouldn't more human beings have common sense?

## 119. PURE CONSCIOUSNESS

Consciousness is awareness and it is manifested as the forms that we think we see and the experiences we believe that we have.

Pure Consciousness is the clearest way that I know to explain the enlightened awareness of Being. When I say pure, I mean no watered down or incomplete idea of consciousness. It is just the real deal.

## 120.  SUMMER IN MY MIND

I love the summer time.  In Southern California where I live, the culture includes long board and body surfing and boogie boarding, sailing, and other water sports, beach volleyball, etc., and a beach lifestyle that is enjoyed by millions of people.

The sun and warmth is what is almost always associated with the summertime. Considering the peaceful feeling that these images create is a great form of contemplation to help get you through the day when you may need a little lift.

## 121.  CONTEMPLATION 4

If you can't actually go to the beach or if you don't have a physical picture of some kind to look at, consider this:
You are sitting on the sand, a lone on the beach, and hearing only the sound of the waves gently crashing onto the shore and the peaceful songs of the seagulls that are flying through the air around you.

You smell the refreshing and cleansing salt water as you breathe. You take normal and deep breaths of the air as you feel comfortable.  You may or may not be conscious of your breathing.

Feel the sand through your toes or as you run your hands through it.

Look into the beautiful blue sky above you. Look at the water and the waves as they naturally form, roll, and break into the shore in orderly rhythmic sets. Contemplate the awesomeness.

## 122. ENLIGHTENMENT

This is an interesting word. It implies that one has arrived in their spiritual journey, but in fact, I think it more practically means that something has awakened within you that realizes something truly profound about life itself.

There can be many definitions of this as well as experiences which is why I will definitely be revisiting this subject and elaborating more. For NOW.... Open your mind to the profundity of the meaning of this word!

## 123. EMPOWERMENT

Everything is complete NOW so that should automatically empower you to do great things and make the most of each moment.

## 124. DON'T SETTLE FOR ANYTHING ELSE

The Universe is complete every moment. There really isn't one moment that is more complete or more perfect than the present moment. Don't settle for anything less than the perfection that is the NOW moment. Remember, it is only illusion if it seems otherwise. Likewise, there can't be anything more than perfection either. I know how real that illusion seems sometimes, but it is just an illusion.

It isn't even possible to actually settle for anything else, more or less than the complete Eternal Universal moment!

## 125. EDUCATION

This word implies that there is a lack that has to be fulfilled, but in fact 'education' isn't what it appears to be. Children are expected to go to school and learn basic concepts in order to function successfully in human society. We all know what most of this is... reading, writing and math also known as arithmetic. I am not questioning the importance of this, just merely discussing the concept of schooling for the purpose of more and better clarification of the definition of education itself.

My point here is you experience schools of learning in many and various ways. Some of the most educated and successful people in the human world didn't even get much if any advanced education in the academic world. Some didn't even graduate from high school.

What actually pans out in your life is exactly what is supposed to happen. That is your educational experience, so-to-speak. If you need to go back to school even as an older adult, the inner voice is very clear about what needs to be done or not done. You are compelled to get whatever it is done when you in fact do listen to that inner voice. At the same time, that inner voice could be what compels you to do the exact opposite of that. As long as you don't succumb to outside pressures that advise you to go to school or to pursue some other avenue of educating oneself without considering what *'you'* genuinely and intuitively feel inside, you are on the right track.

Listen to genuine REAL intuition. The illusive intuition is full of doubt so that is why it is essential to be very clear as you listen. Go into a quiet space with little or no distractions from the outside world and just let your rambling thoughts settle letting life flow naturally. Read the ***Contemplation*** entries in this book if you need some ideas. They might help you.

Everything that you need to know already exists. It is like an invention or even a musician writing a song, for instance. The idea always exists, it's just that at some point someone has to 'uncover it' and let it manifest itself into the world. The educational experience is the same way.

Let it be.

## 126. CONTEMPLATION 5
*Multi-tasking*

There may be those times when you feel like you need to clear the so-called rambling thoughts from your head right NOW, but you have to get some work done at the same time. I believe multi-tasking is the word.

Housework and running errands for instance are often considered mundane tasks, but even while driving (as long as you aren't spaced out) you can be highly aware of your inner silence and even your normal tasks may not seem as tedious, boring, and stressful.

1. Remember to take a few deep breaths as you go about your business and just let the quietness flow through you.

2. Some people like to repeat little phrases to themselves and some just like listening to the silence even amongst the outer noises. Any way that quietness works for you, let that automatically quiet down your thoughts.

This can literally be done anywhere you find yourself... home, work, school, on vacation, doing housework, running errands, etc.

## 127. FAIR

Have you noticed that when you mention the word *fair* in conversation some people think of a community event that usually lasts 2 to 3 weeks or so in a designated area called a fairgrounds?

Have you heard people in conversations then say things like this:

"I've had some horses and pigs entered in the judging when I was a kid." "I love all of the rides and the cotton candy." "Oh, I just go for the fried ice cream and the bacon apple fritters." "There might be a horse race or a great concert in the grandstand on any given day or night that I want to see."

I had to have a little fun there.

When some hear the word *fair* it means something completely different. I have heard comments in conversation that came across something like this:

"I'm sorry, I just don't agree with your statement about equality and that there is enough for everyone because life just isn't fair."

The present MOMENT is fair because all that exists is NOW! NOW can't really be measured in amounts of NOW. It isn't about some people getting more NOW than others. That even sounds absurd. Each moment is always the same NOW. Sometimes, in order to see the world manifest more good things, so-to-speak, we must accept the fact that humans don't really run the Universe and they don't participate in anything REAL that is naturally crafted to serve their own needs more than the needs of other forms of life. Remember, illusion isn't real, but REALITY Is!

### 128.  OCCUPY!

NOW, the present MOMENT, is all we are aware of and the Universe is spaceless and timeless, therefore we can't actually occupy a space or a time, can we?

Can we occupy the present moment?

### 129.  KEEP IT REAL

With all of the phony baloney, superficial, disingenuous, insincerity, and whatever word can be used, it is always refreshing when someone talks to you and keeps it real.  Those moments should be the focus of our attention so that really is a way of life.  Here and Now!

## 130. SPACE OUT

Have you ever been called a space cadet, or even called yourself that?
Haha. Well, space out is a term associated with being a bit dazed,
distracted, and out of it. There's also the terms 'head in the clouds' and 'not
grounded.' Whatever!

Sometimes it is just another way of saying RELAX and don't focus too
much on the problems, just chill! That's how I like to say it.

## 131. Contemplation 6
### *Music*

Sit in an upright position preferably, but if that isn't possible or you just
want to lay down flat, you can do that instead.

Find some nice music that is mellow in some way or another. It doesn't
matter if there are lyrics or not. Obviously if the music does have words, I
suggest lyrics that talk about the inner self, Earth nature, the Universe,
peace, and non-romantic love kind of subject matter. Of course those are my
recommendations, you might feel comfortable with other ideas.

The basic idea is to sit and relax and contemplate being present in the
present MOMENT while you listen.

## 132.  Contemplation 7
*More from Mother Nature and Beyond*

Whenever you are outside in nature make a special effort to pay attention to what is happening around you and even in the heavens beyond.

Closely and attentively observe a hummingbird and the flowers it is attracted to, a butterfly flying around you, a squirrel in a frozen stance or climbing a tree, a rabbit hobbling around the grass, or the neighbor's cat that made it's way into your yard.

Look at the whole of a tree, then specifically focus on a branch, then a sub-branch, then the bark, a leaf or a fruit.

Stare at a beautiful sunset on a partly cloudy night and take in the cloud formations and the magnificent array of colors reflecting off of the clouds.

Stare at a full moon in the sky before the sun has completely set and once again when the sky is completely dark after the sun has set.

Use your imagination as you observe the natural NOW !

## 133.  Floating

Sometimes it may seem like your consciousness is just floating in air or undefined space, but what could possibly be above or below being aware of this moment?

When surfing with a board on a wave or sailing on a boat in the ocean, you have a floating sensation.

Space travelers who go out of the Earth atmosphere float in space where there is no gravity to hold them down.

How could consciousness be above or below itself?  It just Is.  It's that simple really.

## 134. Airwaves

seem to be invisible, yet we are aware of them constantly. We may not always seem to focus on them, but when we do we realize that there really isn't any interruption in the flow of their existence.

## 135. Synchronicity

What happens when in any given moment, you feel like you're on the same wavelength as others? It is a natural thing, because we are always ONE Consciousness.

Human perceptions and the terminology used to describe what it experiences or observes is often what makes the human experience so confusing, challenging, stimulating and interesting simultaneously. This can also be perceived as synchronicity.

Being out of sync is just an appearance. Nothing is actually out of sync in the Universe. The Universe would have to be in chaos if it actually could be out of sync.

Paying attention to the completeness which is the present moment makes Perfect sense.

## 136. Global To Universal

Everything and everyone is essential to the completeness that is the Universe Itself. So when you say that you are a global citizen, that is fine, but you are also saying that you are a citizen of the Universe. One is always essential to the other just like you and myself and everything else.

## 137. Unidentified Flying Objects (UFOs)

You might say that **NOWMAN** comes from outer space and came to the Earth in an unidentified flying object, or that I am an unidentified flying object myself. Well, superheroes usually do fly through the air like a bird, and one can assume that means that I must also be from another galaxy or something. Haha.

Actually, there are unidentified flying objects as well as the identifiable ones according to human legends, beliefs, and perceptions. This may just be how one chooses to perceive what is experienced and observed. The Reality is this....

Everything which is REAL is always identifiable. Just because you and I may not understand something doesn't mean that it is unidentified. Someone or something somewhere must know what an unidentified object actually is or we wouldn't be aware that something exists in the first place. For instance, what you or I call unidentified may be identifiable to a scientist or a Martian.

## 138. Extraterrestrials

Extraterrestrial means anything that exists outside of the Earth and its' atmosphere, so that would mean most of the Universe.
The plurality of that word must mean infinite things that exist as most of the Universe.

It would be natural for us to sometimes feel like extraterrestrials even when living on the surface of the Earth planet because Conscious awareness is actually everything in the Universe this present moment.

### 139. CONTEMPLATION 8

Here's a mantra that could be helpful NOW.

*The Universe is pure Consciousness. It is complete, Infinite, Eternal, Perfect Intelligence. Let all manifestations unfold effortlessly and naturally according to the Universal Order that is Life Itself.*

Letting Life and Its' purpose reveal Itself naturally seems to eliminate stress and the seeming need to personally control. This way, the scattering and meandering thoughts disappear and the clarity is obvious. Let it happen!

### 140. Question for you NOW.

What are you doing for FUN today?

## 141. Signs

Do you see the writing on the wall? Do you see the red flags?

Do you read the signs posted on bulletin boards, at intersections and along the road, or found in the hands of demonstrators at protests?

When you realize that there is a direct message being conveyed, your mind processes it and your inner reaction to it is immediate. The deeper message should then be able to come through loud and clear. The more we are accustomed to paying attention, the more and the faster that we recognize the signs.

## 142. Science!

Science seems to be humankind's best way to analyze what it believes to be the closest thing to proving fact, but what in fact is fact?

I am conscious that science somehow is humankind's form or way of connecting to something greater in the Universe than the human perception and belief systems.

Keep the mind open always!
(and hug a scientist today).

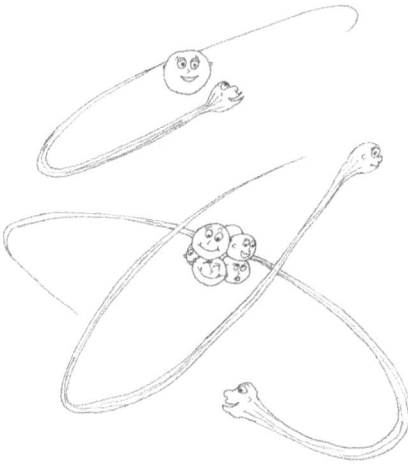

Atoms and Molecules

## 143. CENTER

The center is the middle of something and that is a noun, but what about the verb, *to be centered*? Have you ever found yourself in the center of a room feeling very centered in a state of absolute bliss?

## 144. CONTEMPLATION 9

Find a place as close to the center of the room where you are at the moment and sit in a lotus position with your legs crossed.

Close your eyes and contemplate the existence of absolute bliss.

Don't pay attention to any thoughts that might seem to distract you from feeling centered. Your awareness of the Eternal NOW feels heightened and clear when this is the case.

Enjoy the bliss until you need to go on to another activity.

## 145. ASSEMBLY

We are each individuals in the Universe and in what we refer to as this Earth and human experience.

We are also part of a whole and cannot be individuals without also being part of the whole. We cannot be part of the whole without also being individuals.

This is why we usually feel compelled to join others by participating in group activities together. It is completely natural for us to assemble together because we are social creatures. By that same token, it is absolutely natural to genuinely care about each other when we really consider the purpose for our existence here together on this planet.

## 146. Sovereignty

is a supreme and excellent way of being and living life! That must always be manifested in the present moment.

## 147. Framework:
## Individuals and the Whole

A framework is the basis of how ideas are turned into actions. In order for any worthwhile project or relevant issue to be effective, it must have a strong foundation of moral values with a clear focus of purpose.

In this segment, I am going to talk about the basic framework of how one lives one's life. To elaborate, each one of us is an individual so we must be individually responsible. It is also wise to acknowledge that we as individuals are part of the whole as well.

This framework is a friendly reminder that not only can help keep the ego in check, but be the ongoing basis for humbling ourselves in order to have a better understanding of ourselves as individuals; always part of a whole.

## 148. MOVEMENT

Stay in motion. Keep the mind active by stimulating it with genuine optimism, positive thoughts, challenging ideas, and interesting new experiences!

## 149. MOMENT of RELIEF

If you have had a particularly stressful day, I have some ideas for a little bit of relief. Sometimes it is a good idea to let out some steam with a good hearty laugh, a flow of teardrops, or to verbally vent perhaps to a friend who knows you quite well or to someone who just understands your emotion in that moment. If it is more intense, I suggest something like a punching bag, a pillow, or a beanbag, focus on an intense workout of some kind, a bicycle ride, yoga, or maybe engage in some Tai Chi in the park.

## 150. EGO IN CHECK

Here's a quick little reminder.

Just like taking off your shoes at the door when you enter the house, likewise keep the ego at the door.

## 151. JUSTICE

DO what you know deep inside your consciousness is the right thing and never exclude the other person.

## 152. HOME SWEET HOME

What is the home? There is an expression that says 'home is where the heart is.' What does that mean? There is another saying 'where a man lays his hat is his home.' A house or dwelling may be called a home base. Some people live like gypsies and don't stay in the same place very long. Their concept of home is much different than most families that stay in one house for many years. They adjust to a home base that is often in a state of transition. Kids change schools as well as communities, leave friends behind, and have to make new ones knowing that they may not see those friends left behind ever again. Home takes on a whole different meaning for families that live life this way. Yet all of that being said, some people may live inside a large cardboard box or don't really have a home inside a physical dwelling of any kind, but find their home to be on a street or in various locations that are subjected to the elements.

Living outdoors can be brutally cold in the winter and swelteringly hot in the summer depending on the climate. There is a certain amount of comfort in knowing that there is a home base to come back to one way or another. In this way home does have a sweet sensation, an appeal as something tangible, and in some way is dependable even if it is just 'in the heart.'

## 153. EQUANIMITY

In any moment it is important to pay attention. The human being can often get carried away with their thoughts and actions in the present moment especially if a difficult situation appears. When that seems to be the case, it is very important to be deeply aware of the calm nature that is the existing NOW moment, and stay unaffected by anything that can seem to be going on in or around it. This is why equanimity is essential so that the focus remains on genuine concerns even in more stressful periods of this human experience.

## 154. CONTEMPLATION 10
*Considering equanimity in a challenging situation*

If there is a difficult situation presenting itself in this moment, and you feel a feeling that seems to make you uncomfortable in your own space, so-to-speak, here are a few thoughts to consider:

Close your eyes if you can, but even if you can't, focus solely on the present moment and contemplate how you are essential to the existence of the unlimited Universe which is untouched in this moment of concern.

Whether a few seconds or even a much longer moment, keep that thought of consideration in your mind as long as possible so that the Universe itself through your own sense of calmness and equanimity dispels the tension or the stress. As you find yourself in the next moment, so-to-speak, you realize that you have opened yourself up to the Universe when you discover a sense of relief and perhaps even bliss!

## 155. CONTEMPLATION 11

Fully open mind and consciousness….. NOW!

## 156. CONTEMPLATION 12

*Close your eyes and rest* wherever you can. It is a good exercise when you have had an extra busy day, you feel drained, and the brain needs a little relief.

## 157. CONTEMPLATION 13

Listen…………………

## 158. Open Mic

Expressing oneself in front of a large captive audience isn't a personal thrill of the ego when it is backed with the fervor of passion, especially when it comes to deeply addressing social issues and matters of simple and profound compassion.

## 159. CONTEMPLATION 14

Observe the faces of those around you.   Smile and see what happens.

## 160.  CRITICAL MASS

Has a crisis accelerated to a point where there can be no more denial that something must be done in order to alleviate a deep problem?

Does there then seem to be a rush for some function or task to be completed or problem to be solved and what will be the outcome of the resolution?

When you see how crowds or groups of people can seem to be dysfunctional, it is easy to be critical of the masses.

## 161. RELATIVE

We are all related because we live on the planet Earth. What does it mean to be related by blood? How about genetics? What does relativity actually mean? Are we related by brainwaves and energy?

## 162. ORGANIZATION

Organizing is needed to complete certain tasks successfully. An organization of tasks must first be determined as tasks so that the tasks can be completed. It requires more than one person to call something an organization. One thing is certain... when something needs to happen and a task must be completed, the focus must be the present moment.

## 163. TRANSPORTATION

Do we really move from one place to another when we walk, ride a bicycle or train, drive a vehicle, or fly in aircraft?
Whatever you choose to believe is fine, and one thing is for sure. NOW is all that exists and that is what is most important when you are in motion.

## 164. CONTEMPLATION 15

Sometimes we can be so passionate about something and work so much on a time consuming project or endeavor of some sort, that we feel large amounts of stress and just need to stop for a moment. Once you stop and by that I mean stop letting the thoughts keep wandering, you will be in the frame of mind to really open up consciousness through continued contemplation, meditation or whatever works for you.

## 165. NOTHING?

I heard someone say tonight that *'I am nothing.'* It is important to be humble, but the truth of the matter is, each of us is something because we are conscious that we exist and that we are conscious... right NOW!

## 166. CONTEMPLATION 16

Purely and simply.... All that exists is the present moment. Consider how simple it is and how pure that simplicity always is. The present moment can never be interrupted when we are focused only on that purely simple fact.

## 167. SATISFACTION

Are you pleased with how you have and are currently living your life? Looking at the present moment would you say that you are happy? Genuine happiness is satisfaction.

## 168. MESSAGE AND THE MESSENGER

The message and the messenger are ONE and the same. The focus must be the message however because without the message there would be no need for the messenger.

## NOWMAN ONE LINERS

**169.** Each moment is inspirational just because each moment exists.

**170.** Don't worry about the partners of the future or dwell on the enemies of the past because NOW is your present friend!

**171.** When living and being aware of only the present moment you can't be afraid of going too deep or concern yourself with being too shallow.

**172.** A true friend doesn't bail on you or withdraw their love from you... you can bank on that!

**173**. Education is the ongoing understanding of our roles as essential parts of the Universe.

**174.** What I feel is what I know!

**175.** Have you ever written a poem that included the words comb, dome, foam, home, gnome, or roam?

**176**. Not every book has a table of contents, but reading a good book does provide a certain amount of contentment.

**177**. NOW is Eternal just like HERE is Infinite.

**178.** This current moment isn't mysterious because you know that you are present in it NOW.

**179.** One of the most basic and fundamental realizations is the fact that *love one another* is an essential part of one's effective daily life routine and focus.

**180.** The present moment is Eternal so it doesn't really matter if you perceive something that seems temporal.

**181.** An inspired revelation can appear in an instant and then seem to drastically change the way we personally view the world or how the world views itself.

**182.** The word *union* is associated with all kinds of things from labor to marriage, but it always means some kind of togetherness.

**183.** A true friend understands that time is not relevant because the genuine connection is always instantaneous and in the present moment.

**184.** Some people call middle age the middle of life, but that is no more true than the month of June is the middle of Eternity.

**185.** There are four seasons, but the moment is really the only focus of our attention NOW regardless of the climate.

**186. REAL TIME**

There is no such 'thing' as time, but what's REAL does exist!

**187.** Blog Excerpt # 5

**Daylight savings time... what is time? All that exists is............NOW!**

## 188. Contemplation 17

Consider this: NOW really isn't influential because it is constant and always existing so nothing can actually exist outside of the present moment for it to influence. Paying attention by quiet consideration of the Eternal NOW in the present makes it clearly apparent that Enlightenment is what you are actually experiencing even as you read this.

## 189. ALL

This word takes into account anything and everything. It is synonymous with the Universe.

## 190. SOCIAL

All creatures have social functions in collective living situations. In the human world, we hear expressions like 'no man is an island,' 'united we stand and divided we fall,' 'we all are one,' and 'common good.' This would certainly indicate for the most part that we aren't hermits. We actually thrive on social activities. It is therefore sensible that human beings would care for other life... humans, animals, and mother nature herself. Understanding this in the present moment surely proves that.

## 191. BECOMING

What could you become if everything exists in the present moment?

## 192. Question: What is the purpose of existence?

NOWMAN: I always like to say that the purpose of this life is to love each other and also to have fun!

If that is where I'm supposed to be, then I Am there now.

## 193. Anonymous

I don't know who said that when and why let alone what it means. Or maybe I do know, but I just can't say.

## 194. CLICHES

A cliché is one of those words that is both a noun and a adjective, but it originated from a root word that's actually a verb. Cliché usually refers to predictable. Why be predictable in ways that aren't crucial and unpredictable in ways that are most important to the good of the whole? I once heard a college commencement speaker say something like this and I paraphrase: "When you go into the world, don't be mediocre, always strive for excellence in whatever good that you do." The belief that one must always dwell on material things for success let alone survival could be perceived as a cliché, but to simply **Love each other** which also may seem to be a cliché, is truly essential to real success and survival, as I see it.

## 195. TRANSPARENCY

This word means to be completely open and honest. Total clarity so as to allow respect and trust to manifest. Human beings must learn to genuinely accept this kind of behavior and of course there is also responsibility to respect the sanctity of the privilege. It is part of the reason that humans are having this human experience. Why deny it? Embrace it NOW!

## 196. THE FLOW

Have you heard the expression 'GO WITH THE FLOW?' There is a lot of Truth in that statement. It is a natural flow, of course. Open the mind and just let your thoughts go free. Keep your mind focused and you'll experience how natural it is to live in the present moment with ease and purpose. Be free yet focused.

## 197. LOVE DISARMS

A story was told about a man who was having mental distress; yelling obscenities, being a bit aggressive and perhaps obnoxious when people were approaching him for the purpose of trying to talk to him and help him. A woman came forward and advised the men gathered around that she had been talking to this man for several days and felt compelled to reach out to him in this moment. Many people were standing around and observing as this woman spoke to the man in a calm and gentle voice. Even though no one heard what was actually being said in an exchange of dialogue, the man stopped yelling altogether, suddenly broke into sobs, and then went down to his knees. You are free to interpret what this story means. I see it as definitive love in action at the core of the purpose for life!

## 198. JOY!

Happiness is a way of life and joy is the main byproduct.

## NOWMAN ONE LINERS

**199.** Perfect Love eliminates fear... instantaneously!

**200.** A live stream, webcam, or other kinds of live or pre-recorded broadcasts are several ways that you can pretend to be in more than one place at the same moment.

**201.** Listen to the silence... for contemplation and relaxation.

**202.** Compassion... everyone can seem to be in need, one way or another.

**203.** A university philosophy professor once created an essay test with one question; only one word on a piece of paper that said 'Why?' and I know for a fact that one of the students wrote 'why not?' underneath it. I believe he got an A grade, also.

**204.** An election is usually associated with politics, but I see it as a choice, and I choose to be free rather than restricted.

**205.** We must have hope, but hope isn't limited to what the ego seems to believe that it is.

**206.** A hug is a perfect way to show direct love to someone without having to even say a word.

**207.** Belief is usually accompanied by faith, fact is usually accompanied by proof, and love is just what it is.

**208.** The NOW moment doesn't have to be on the offensive or the defensive because it doesn't take the initiative or need to be passive, it's just being constantly the present.

**209.** Why waste your time thinking that you have to have power especially over other human beings or other living things when it's just like money; you can't take it with you?

**210.** A comfort zone is a place where you'll hopefully realize that you can't always be comfortable with old habits.

**211.** I have been asked what planet that I came from and I always say... the Earth of course unless I feel like making that individual asking the question believe that I really am from Mars or something.

**212. CONTEMPLATION 18**
There's an incredible feeling in the air and I really feel alive!

**213.** The present moment can never disrupt itself; that just isn't possible.

**214.** Did you get the memo at the office referencing the memo about the memo circulating around that says that the memo is about how to make sure the memo that you are reading says to discard the original memo?

**215.** Do you sometimes or even frequently wish someone to have 'pleasant dreams' in the evening time before going to bed at night?

**216.** Fast forward and rewind, like the past and future, are illusive. Once the illusions disappear, and they will, the genuine nature of the present moment is the only thing to actually be aware of.

**217.** Whenever in doubt, NOW is the genuine article, the proof of the existence of something in the present moment.

**218. UNION**

Union means togetherness in one form or another. Be loyal to what you know in your heart that is truly inclusive of the whole and not exclusively self-serving whether it is an individual concern or even the agenda of an organization of some kind. Seek the deeper meaning than what is on the surface. Self-serving to not include others is not union; it is division. Don't give attention to division and ACT always to acknowledge the ONENESS of living NOW!

## 219. CONTEMPLATION 19

Close your eyes.
Lay on the floor or sit upright with good posture in a chair.
Try to think about absolutely nothing in complete silence.
NOW consider the meaning of pure consciousness.
Continue this contemplation so that your mind stays fully open
to the meaning of pure consciousness always manifesting
itself. Stay silent for at least as long as it takes to feel some
kind of natural euphoria.

## 220. PAY ATTENTION

It will come in handy one day to pay attention to facts and not
focus on beliefs.
Do not judge by appearances but discern the best ways that
your heart and head do actually work together.
Don't be surprised if you discover that the confidence that you
are right and the other person is wrong might actually be more
accurate stating it the other way around.

## NOWMAN ONE LINERS

### 221.
While one should not deny human responsibilities, why be
dominated by them?

### 222.
If you believe that Life is Eternal and continues after human
death, for the sake of consistency, wouldn't you have to
believe that Life preceded human birth?

### 223.
There must be more than dualism, seeing existence in twos, as
binary, double, and twice, etc. because it all comes together as
one Universe.

### 224. LUKE WARM
The mind set that came up with left, right, and center must
have also created the concept of hot, warm and cold.

**225.**
Who ever said that life would be easy, but it would be
reasonable for life to be easier.

**226.**
An example of hope manifesting is when a sleeping giant
starts to wake up.

**227.**
Have you ever been in a social environment with a lot of people
in it and almost everyone that you approach is a total stranger
yet you can speak to them, and even start a spontaneous
conversation with very little effort?

**228.**
The ego is a perfect example of how human beings can believe
that they are illusively better, more accurate with facts, more
deserving, successful, and entitled than others, and justify
virtually any illusive reason why this delusion is true.

**229.**
Sometimes humans are obsessed with attracting attention and
will use all sorts of ways to make themselves *stand out* from
the crowd.

**230.**
Have you ever made what you believed to be an extra effort to
not forget something and then you forget that very thing that
you made the effort to try not to forget?

**231.**
Don't settle for mediocrity, you are better than that!

**232.**
Keeping the mind open is like recognizing that what is
considered early to someone means late to another person.

**233.**
A true humanitarian knows what needs to be done when there is a specific human need to be attended to or issue to be resolved, depending on that individual's area of expertise of course.

**234.**
Have you ever noticed that the pronunciations of the sounds *ummm* or *ahhh* seem to show up and mean the same thing in all languages? (source of reference: subtitles in films)

**235.**
Moving forward NOW still means that NOW is the moment of that happening.

**236.**
Free speech is when you can freely speak what you want in a public or private space or at least that is how it was originally understood.

**237.**
*Question:* If there was just one word to describe it all what would that one word be?   *Answer:* Universe.

**238.**
Co-dependency implies insecurity. Interdependency implies cooperation working together.  Independency implies total freedom.

**239.  The Wind**

The wind blows and we really don't know the origin of it or exactly where it is going.  We just feel it go across our face or body when we are physically confronted by it.  When we hear it, we have no idea about its' direction unless we look at tree branches or something like that.

It seems invisible and yet we do see and sometimes hear evidence of it. Right now, it is blowing outside my windows, and it sounds like it might be moving as fast as 80 miles an hour at times.  Hmmm. How is that measured?  Someone figures that stuff out.  Any way you look at it (if you can actually look at wind) everything exists in the NOW and the only place to discover it, is here.

## 240.  Affinity

What do you like about something or someone when you feel a natural attraction of some kind?  What is it that we often share in common with people, things, or even geographical places? The word affinity is one of those words with a profound meaning as we better understand how to connect with one another.   This is an aspect that I believe is part of the so-called human evolutionary development or experience.  We are social creatures so it is natural to want to connect with others who are like-minded. These kinds of spontaneous and natural relationships are what often bring a lot of joy and enrichment into our lives. For instance, how can you not be attracted to simple genuine love?

## 241.   EVICTION

When someone serves you an eviction notice to vacate the premises, it isn't actually possible to be evicted from being present in the present MOMENT.

## 242.  PAYMENTS DUE

When you make up-to-date payments NOW due on a bill you would be current.  Would that mean that there really isn't any such thing as past due or a future due date because the past is past and that next due date seems to be in the future when actually all that exists is the present moment?

## 243. CONTEMPLATION 20

Without just staring for the sake of staring, look out a window at some object in nature... maybe just a tree leaf or one single pedal on a flower.  Use your imagination. Focus on that for a while until it is clear that you are aware of the simple beauty.

That observation turns into a real experience within your consciousness.

## 244. GIVING THANKS

There is a day that is celebrated in some places for the purpose of giving thanks. There are specific traditions that accompany any holiday and this one is certainly no exception. Why limit the massive public awareness to just this one day? This general attitude is something that more and more people are celebrating and focusing on every day and it should be a priority even moment to moment. Being grateful is not just a normal thing, it also makes you feel great about life even when life seems to have many undesirable elements in it. There are always things, circumstances and especially people to be thankful for.

## 245. CONTEMPLATION 21
### Giving Thanks

Here and NOW is a constant thing or idea to be aware of. As you quietly consider this, keep the mind silently focused on being thankful for all good each moment until you feel clear about how awesome and all encompassing this is. When you are finished in your quiet space, then go out and meet people and see how it impacts the way that you talk to others and even total strangers. You can also keenly observe how they speak to you.

## 246. Together NOW!

We are all one in this one Universe. We are always together NOW!

## 247.  What is LAW?

There is Principle and Order in the Universe and we are obligated to pay attention to and be the living manifestation of the ethical Principle. If there seems to be a man-made rule of law that doesn't follow the Principle, then we must turn our whole attention to the Law of the Universe because the Law of the Universe is Reality and not illusion.  Even when we follow so-called man-made laws, we must recognize the Principle existing or we are caught up in an illusion.

To put it simply... Things are not what they appear to be.  Stay focused on Reality while not denying illusion, but don't get caught up in the illusion. Illusion isn't real.

This present moment is REAL.... NOW!

## 248.  LIKE and LOVE

What difference is there really between like and love?  Is love a more intense or intimate like?  Can you make like to someone and can you love someone but not like that one?   I suppose any combination would be possible in the Universe of possibilities.
Words are just semantics anyway. The feeling or deeper meaning behind a word is what is most important, don't you think?

## 249. Nowman Blog:
## HOW ABOUT MAKE THE SEASON JOLLY WITH 'TIS THE REASON TO END FOLLY?'

At this time of the year that traditionally starts with Black Friday, the day after another holiday called Thanksgiving, of course the marketplace is bombarded with the hype of mass consumerism. We hear and see stories of customer frenzy over deals on big price breaks with the expectation for a big season of big profits for many of the big corporations.

Then every January, we continue to hear the disappointing news of lower sales than originally hoped for during the entire season. Economists continue to speculate what the reasons are as they analyze their statistics which continue to be dismal in most markets. Is it any real surprise?

Many people that I know are legitimately broke and not because they just don't know how to handle money or keep a job on their own accord. As more and more people continue to lose their jobs, their homes, pensions and other benefits, therefore lose more opportunities to build personal capital for what are considered more secure futures in the so-called established free market system, the more frugal that they will become especially at the time of the year known as 'the most wonderful time of the year;' quoting that famous classic holiday song.

Fewer gifts with higher price tags are being purchased and even credit cards are used much more sparingly these days.

Consumer confidence continues to wane, but that doesn't mean that people have completely given up on gift giving and sharing. It's quite the contrary actually. There are many people who always give their time and in other ways to charity all year around even though organizations such as food banks definitely feel the economic crunch when they have to put out extra appeals for donations of more goods and volunteer services at various times of the year.

We as consumers will continue to consume, but we must decide what we really want to consume. How about instead of being obsessed with consumer goods produced by cheap labor and sold for exorbitant prices, that we participate in socially and economically responsible gift giving that truly and deeply touches our hearts and shows respect for human beings as we reach out and care for each other? That is supposed to be what gift giving is about, but is that on people's minds when they go to a store with pepper spray to get to the front of the line, or even just fill their carts with a lot of stuff that will eventually just sit in storage somewhere because of sentimental but no real practical value? It doesn't even really help the economy or the physical and social environments as we as a global society are seeing and realizing more and more.

How about buying environmentally friendly and personal wellness gifts such as organic foods and other health conscious products or even yoga sessions and bicycles? How about supporting locally owned mom and pop shops? How about exchanging hand crafted or other homemade gifts? How about more bartering? I know a meet-up group that is actually doing a secret Santa online by just sending creative e-mail cards and greetings with happy messages.

Some of the best times in my life have just been being with wonderful loving people and enjoying their company and conversation. It makes me feel very jolly just thinking about it.

Some of the best gifts are free or don't require much if any money at all. This is as good a time as any to make a statement that we care about our fellow human beings to the point that we aren't going to focus attention on the extreme materialism of our culture. Many of us love our country and the planet where we live. We just have a great need as I see it to really understand and act on our most important priorities. NOW is a good time to focus more on the reason to be jolly rather than all of the needless folly. Enjoy the celebrations NOW and all year long.

Love and Peace NOW...
From NOWMAN

(NOWMAN blog from November 2011)

## 250. DRAMA
Life seems to be the appearance of acting out a drama on some kind of surreal stage. No matter what the perception, angle, ideology, or storyline. It is all just fabrication. The living in the moment is reality and the drama that appears in the moment is not.

## 251. MEDIA

Written or photographed, on line or on paper, visual or audio, it is just a vehicle to get a message out. Some of those messages seem to have more substance than others. You are reading a form of media right now. Make it a form of edutainment.

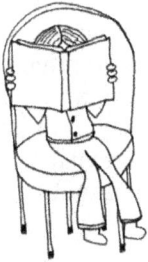

## OCCUPY OUTREACH: WHAT KINDS OF GIFTS DO WE GIVE TO EACH OTHER?

Just think of it. The Occupy Movement has given the world a great amazing and unique gift. Just yesterday, I had a conversation with a friend about how just one picture of tents in Zuccotti Park or on the lawn of L.A. City Hall was a beautiful thing showing the world that people can peacefully assemble to address their grievances as guaranteed in the U.S. Constitution. As we all know, there were probably millions of pictures, videos, and various visuals from the first phase of Occupy between September and December.

Any movement like this, just like a human being, has to grow from infancy into maturity. Even the United States is the new kid on the block in the world of history and yet many have said worldwide that it became the most interesting experiment of governance in the history of the world. Occupy has shown us how to revisit that infancy in many ways, and how we all must mature, a subject that I hope to revisit as time goes on. For now, what kind of gift is the Occupy Movement?

As human beings tend to be, there are going to be growing pains. Some people will go through those growing pains differently than others causing some friction once in a while. Here is where we see a lot of the gift. We are giving it to each other when we disagree with each other as much if not more than when we agree with each other. We learn through solidarity of cause in that we really have a lot more in common than we are different from one another. What a beautiful gift. I am working with loving people from all walks and experiences in life and in every part of my life. I feel very enriched and very blessed.

Occupy has gotten a lot of people's attention. Some of that attention is focused on negativity when there are some clashes in egos, personalities, belief systems and priorities even in actions pertaining to the movement. It's like the Charles Dickens' classic tale and sometimes we have to deal with the 'bah humbugs' from the Scrooges of the world. This is when we realize that some of those differences can seem greater than we thought.

We learn to process those feelings somehow and we move on and stay focused on the bigger purpose. Again, some process those feelings faster than others. Part of that solidarity is embracing patience, but sometimes we all must set the ego aside for the benefit of the greater Good.

This is just the beginning. Going back to my conversation with my fellow activist brother. Our greatest gifts are what we all can bring and will continue to bring to the world that we live in.... that is the gift of the Holiday that cannot be replaced by material things. That is the gift that we give to each other, to others in the community, and literally all around the world.

What kinds of gifts do we give to each other? We can simply give of ourselves to each other....as long as how we give and what we give is GOOD!
This is just to start.

Love and Peace NOW,
NOWMAN
(NOWMAN blog from December 2011)

## 253. NOWMAN BLOG:
## OCCUPYING CONSCIOUSNESS IN A NEW ERA!

This is the time of year that we seem to say goodbye to a year and welcome in a new one. So, what is the big deal, really now? There's nothing wrong with celebrating this, but is it really necessary to make a big deal out of it?
While some people talk about their New Year's parties, resolutions that they probably won't keep, and all the business as usual, I keep thinking about all of the people losing their homes and tent cities of homeless people around the world. This is just a microcosm of a deep, deep problem that totally engulfs our world at this moment. Many of us are no longer in denial of that.

Whatever you think about Nostradamus, the Age of Aquarius, Apocalypse, or any concept of genuine Enlightenment, millions of people are very eager for some great news about the state of the world.

How about occupying Consciousness?  I like that idea.  Try to wrap
your mind around that one for a while and then we can engage in
more conversation.

No New Year's resolutions for me and I am not dwelling on that end
of the world stuff either.  Reach out to others and engage in relevant
dialogue.

Happy and prosperous New Year to you!
Get ready to occupy Consciousness.
We are moving into a new era.

Love and Peace NOW!
NOWMAN

(NOWMAN blog from December 2011)

## 254.  PARADE

Is a parade just a celebration of folly in the streets or can a greater
message be conveyed under the guise of frivolity?  I'd like to think
that the latter is more the truth.  The truth does set us free, but
freedom is something that we claim to already have, so why don't we
just use it?  Change is direly needed NOW! We choose peaceful
change and change is inevitable.  How is this message communicated
more effectively at a critical time?

## MORE NOWMAN SHORTS

**255.** *Revolution* is a word usually associated with change that could implicate aggressive behavior, but even that word can mean gentle behavior and peaceful change just as it can also mean that a planet is in an orbit around a sun.

How about a revolution of the heart?

**256. EDUTAINMENT** is a word sometimes used to describe the combination of education and entertainment that can seem like an oxymoron unless you are referring to the combination of effective education with good art.

**257. RULE OF LAW**
The rule of law is national and in the U.S.A. and the free world, is part of everyone's true constitutional rights in a democratic political system. That being said, Universal Law always trumps manmade law.

**258. INTERNET**
Technology can change the world of appearances. The Internet is a prime example of how radical change is in fact peaceful when we embrace it.

**259. WORLD WIDE WEB**
What a brilliant concept that alludes to the idea that we are all one, equal, and together in a web of information and ideas.

**260. SCHOOL OF LIFE**

We are constantly learning whether we pay attention or not. Life itself is a school that is naturally showing us who we are each moment. The question is... are we paying attention to that constant demonstration?

**261. INSTANTANEOUS**

*Spontaneity in the moment* could be one of the definitions for instantaneous.

**262. WHAT? WHY? HOW?**

These questions are just the beginning of how we identify ideas so that we can frame them. Framing is a method which makes the ideas presentable in such a manner that the description is easier for the audience, whom the ideas are intended for, to grasp and understand. Once we have determined that we have a concept, an event, an action, or are developing an idea to grow it into some kind of manifestation, we have started to frame it. We can say that once we have completed this process initially that we have in fact officially framed it. This means that we have acknowledged the existence of an identity of some kind and then have given it a label only in order to attempt to better identify it and explain it.

**263. FRAMING AN IDEA**

**For an example:**

*What?* We need peaceful yet radical change in a dysfunctional system of economic injustice.

*Note:* How do we clearly and definitively communicate this idea without watering down the meaning or creating fear that seems to numb and cause inaction? This is where transparency does come into the picture. No more over simplification of complex issues, confusion about black and white and gray as we identify the priorities, and denial of critical issues. The moment is NOW!

*Why?* Success is vital for survival of our planet and all of our species.

*Note:* This isn't an extreme point of view. The eco-system is in peril and humanity itself seems to be on the brink of some kind of major paradigm shift.

*How?* Repeat constructive actions over and over again by being transparent and loving towards everyone including strangers wherever you meet them.

## 264. ARTICULATE THE VISION!

As I was wrapping my brain around the contemplation of a new year beginning, my awareness was heightened to the fact of how social media plays a major part in the communication and intrigue of a changing world. We also live in a world on this Earth planet that is in dire need of major redemption, healing, revelation and all sorts of hopeful genuine and productive manifestations. I realize that most discussion should be focused on starting a new era as we always move forward cognizant and aware of always living in the moment NOW!

I marched incognito at the front of a unique parade with about a thousand people that immediately followed an internationally famous parade with hundreds of thousands of people in the audience from all over the world watching from the street and in huge grandstands built along the street. I saw looks of bewilderment that spoke volumes to me; revealing where many people are right now in their understanding of how serious our global and personal crises actually are.

Even a friend of mine tells me that he is following what is going on with the global awakening, but is personally still complacent and uncertain about what it all means beyond the idea that a lot of people are peacefully protesting because they aren't working, can't find work, or are upset and no longer in denial of something.

I find that the expanding experience of humans reaching out to their fellow humans as equals continues to be the most intriguing part of the social phenomenon that has emerged in our changing world.

The dialogue in my most recent meet up focused on the subject of being role models for others who remain curious, but aren't really engaged in being pro active, and for critics who are still skeptical about looking at something other than what is actually perceived as status quo. The discussion continued with the ideas that each one of us is an individual role model and together we are collective role models.

Because of the movements worldwide, I do see more and more recognition of the fact that we are a part of each other because so many barriers and over inflated egos that have seemingly separated us are now in the process of being broken down. The more that this becomes a part of our daily routines, the more this message will touch the hearts and lives of those we come in contact with personally and through social media. By fulfilling our true purpose starting with the basic fundamentals of human compassion, we automatically practice economic and social justice and are leading by example.

This is the basic beginning of many discussions as we articulate our thoughts. The framing of any movement's vision includes the inspiration of current events through our direct actions as groups as well as how our daily lives connect us to each another.

Love and Peace NOW!
NOWMAN

(NOWMAN blog from December 2011)

## 265. IMAGINATION!

Imagination is what opens the mind and speaks through the heart. Our lives should be full of imagination. We should use that energy which we call the creative energy to change the world around us every possible moment.

## 266. NUTRITION MOMENT:
The Kinds of Nutrition

There are emotional, mental, and physical attributes of nutrition.

I see it all as Spiritual nutrition....NOW!

## 267. NUTRITION MOMENT:
Yerba Mate

I recently discovered a new herb in tea form that is called yerba mate and it comes from the yerba mate tree and was first discovered by the Ache Guayaki people of the sub-tropical rainforests of Paraguay, Argentina, and Brazil. It contains 24 vitamins and minerals, 15 amino acids, and lots of anti-oxidants.
Wow! Mother Nature is truly amazing, isn't she? We should always be cognizant of the natural world and pay attention to the life giving qualities instead of trying to force our egotistical and greedy interests onto it.

## 268. NUTRITION MOMENT:
THE MOMENT NOW

Who knows what natural hormones may be stimulated in the physical body when our focus is clear and centered on living in the Eternal moment NOW?

## 269. CONTEMPLATION 22
Nutrition and More!

Close your eyes where you are now. Consider how the Universe consists of all sorts of substances that are directly and immediately a part of your existence. Include the idea of nutrition, wellness as it is also called, and what enriches the physical body and your entire being as it is essential to the Universe Itself. Part of that recognition is that everyone and everything makes up the consistency of the Universe. Let the illusion just fade away and peacefully feel the Reality of *being* here and NOW!

## 270. SUSTAINABILITY

Sustenance, maintenance and consistency are very important when we activate the practical meanings of those words in our day-to-day lives. It makes sense to always desire and experience a high quality of life. A genuinely high quality of life is not based on materiality and greed, or in other words, the kind of behavior that traditionally encourages and causes imbalance in the distribution and access to as well as the waste of available and valuable resources. We must and WE WILL create a truly sustainable global way of life.

## 271. LIVE STREAMING

Live streaming is genuine and uncensored, the real deal, and the real raw news. What a great social media phenomenon.

## 272. WHAT IS FAITH?

Do you have faith in a human perception about the meaning of life, the purpose of existence itself? Contemplate this for a moment. What does it mean to have faith in something that you honestly know nothing about or have no actual facts to base a conclusion upon? Faith is the evidence of things not seen is one definition. That is profound, but how many humans really understand what 'things not seen' actually refers to? Things not seen to me would be *Consciousness* that doesn't manifest itself in some kind of physical form as we are used to perceiving in this human experience. It would still somehow be tangible without having to be attached to some specific form that is experienced through one or a combination of five human senses.
Do you have faith in intelligence existing in the Universe?
Contemplate that one for a while.

## 273. "I'm Hungry."

Has someone said this to you lately? Maybe you've heard it from someone on the street. I say this every day even when my belly is full. Our minds as well as our bodies need what I will call nourishment, also.

I'm not talking about feeding the ego. Most people have no problem with that one. That kind of energy is better spent elsewhere.

Read a book, share your life with others, have new experiences that broaden your view of this human experience that you are here to participate in without just focusing on yourself. This satisfies the hunger and you'll want more and more and the satisfaction doesn't stop!

**274.   Note to David DeGraw (One of the original organizers of the 99% Movement & Occupy Wall Street)**

The Occupy Wall Street Movement coming into manifestation is the first time in my life that I really felt the genuine oneness of the whole of humankind on this Earth planet.  The passion and the true empowerment of that revelation not only continues to drive me to further deepen my ethical values and roots, but to also use all of my talents and skills, and to seek out others even more who share this passion and desire to be an active part of a global consciousness that at its' core is focused on genuine love and justice for all.  The phenomenon of the new relationships continues to inspire and challenge while keeping the ego in check.   This whole experience will surely evolve into something beyond anything that we can currently envision, but our mission can no longer be denied in this present moment NOW as we go forward. [1]

**275. DISCERNMENT**

This is a word whose meaning must be considered very carefully.  First of all, I think it is important to talk about what it DOESN'T MEAN.  It isn't a form of censorship that insists that it is always right and must exclude certain points of view and individuals and groups, for that matter, because it is 'a personal point of view.'

This is another subject that requires real check and balance of the ego.  What one person may feel passionate about, another may not or not as much.
What one may feel is a highly moral and/or ethical issue, another one may feel that it is not.
Herein lies the difficulty in even defining this term let a lone acting on it in a constructive manner.

Using personal judgment comes into play here and that in some circles becomes an area of avoidance because of the controversy that it automatically creates.  Situations exist when decisions have to be made and that is why democracy is used in those situations especially where more than just a few people are involved in some kind of decision-making.

----

[1] Quote also from David DeGraw's Open Mic of 'The Economic Elite Vs. the People of the United States of America' – ampedstatus.com

However, three is a crowd, as the expression goes, and when you have issues that deal with the masses, a lot of this dialogue gets thrown out of the window because it is deemed that it just takes too much time and is impossible to maneuver when decisions have to be made in a timely fashion, for instance.

The one bit of advice that I can suggest from my experience is to take a DEEP and LONG look at one's ego before making decisions that involve other people... I have had to make decisions that involved one other person directly to an indefinite number of people directly to millions indirectly. The principle is the same. I had to ask myself 'what is really the most important for the common good of ALL involved?' Then I proceeded to make my decisions to the best of my ability on that pretext (see the *Contemplation for Discerning Rightful Actions* for some ideas).

Wow, I just used a lot of wordage in this stream of consciousness just NOW. It is from the heart and that comes from a place that is well thought out and deeply cares about YOU!

## 276. Contemplation 23
Discerning Rightful Actions

What is the first consideration of myself in this issue or situation that I am pondering? Is it truly of vital importance to consider it in a certain way? In other words, is it a matter of life and death (as the expression goes)?

How does this consideration fit into the perceptions of those around me? Likewise would it be considered a matter of life and death?

How does this consideration fit into the perceptions of the even bigger picture if that is a relevant point of clarification?

So the obvious questions to determine relevance have been asked. NOW.... If it isn't a matter of life and death, then does it have a purpose that goes beyond egos and personalities?

If yes, then quietly contemplate the next course of action in light of the most impersonal approach that you can possibly open yourself up to.

If no, forget it. Move on... NEXT.

## NOWisms

**277.** The ego can seem to marginalize the relevant message. Humility gives the messenger of that relevant message a purpose to be that messenger.

**278.** Simplify the ways that you communicate however you can, but don't marginalize the message in the process.

**279.** How many times have you heard someone say something like this:

"I needed this done yesterday."

Chill out... that was yesterday. This is NOW!

**280.** Some people can talk a lot, but they say nothing. Sometimes people talk a little and say nothing. Sometimes a person that talks a lot says a lot of relevant things and you find yourself trying to wrap your brain around it to better understand what you just heard. Sometimes, we try to wrap our brains around just one simple statement. Sometimes statements are so simple and profound that we can miss the meaning at first.

**281.** Huh?

**282.** Sometimes I feel ornery and as long as what happens is innocent, playful, peaceful, doesn't violate someone's space and isn't something really illegal, unethical or something, I say just use common sense in your decision to act.

**283.** Everyone may not have a story to share so-to-speak, but everyone has an experience they're living.

**284.** Money and egos.... These two things could disappear now and I honestly wouldn't miss them.

**285.** If I believe in a fact which I talk about, am I speaking factually?

**286.** A *channel* is a term used to describe the entity that carries messages through the airwaves. It also can be used to identify a waterway. Some psychics use it as a verb when they portray some kind of messenger from another place and time that speaks through them.

The word philosophically pertains to some kind of avenue for information or to anything in general that we want or need access to.

**287.** Do you ever get this feeling that you are walking around in a dream because it all just seems so unreal?

**288.** Have you ever been told that you have an attitude problem by someone who just seems to want to argue with you and might even ask you what *your* problem is?

**289.** The message is always more important than the messenger, but there has to be the messenger for the message. Maintain the integrity of what that means!

**290.** When the message is definitely important, you don't want to marginalize the messenger of that message, even if that messenger may annoy you in some way.

**291.** Most people have good intentions, but are stuck on something that seems to hold back what could be called their Spiritual progress. Maybe it's the primary focus or over-emphasis on money, organized religion, emotional relationships, or any number of distractions from what is truly most important in this life.

**292.** Stay decentralized and humble. In other words, try not to think that you have it all figured out. This behavior maintains sanity.

**293.** Be a leader, but don't think you're the only leader...ever!

**294.** Negative attitudes are not productive, but by the same token what good does the banter of unrealistic optimism do?

**295.** When someone has an abundance of love to share why should that one not want to generously share that love with as many people as possible?

**296**. When someone has an abundance of money to share, why should that one not want to generously share that money with as many people as possible?

**297**. When someone has an abundance of numerous resources to share, why should that one not want to generously share those resources with as many people as possible?

**298.** Being part of a grassroots movement literally means that you have to be grounded in your principles and always keep moving!

**299. ENGAGEMENT**
Now is always the time to get engaged and I don't mean the engagement that leads to matrimony.

**300.** When you go to your job, do you see that as an occupation?

**301.** February is the month that includes a day dedicated to romantic love and the birthdates of two U.S. Presidents. It is also when the ground hog comes out either to see or to not see its' shadow. I don't have a punch line here, but there must be a joke somewhere. Have a great day!

**302. The Holiday of NOW!**
Here's something fun you can do if you get bored. Create an idea for a new Holiday that could be celebrated anywhere. For example: Every day can be the NOW DAY. I like that idea. Let's celebrate that NOW!

**FUN WITH WORDS AND ACRONYMS**

**303.** Likely About Understanding Great Humor  (LAUGH)
**304.** Something Making Issues Less Extreme    (SMILE)
**305.** Having Optimistic Plans Engaged         (HOPE)
**306.**  OMIF
Open Mouth Insert Foot
**307.**  DGT
Don't Go There
**308.**  WYHBRTW

Wash your hands before returning to work
**309.** AYKM?
Are you kidding me?
**310.** TLTW
Too lazy to write
**311.** WTF?
Where's the FUN?
**312.** BWNN
Band With No Name
**313.** ABCD
First four letters of the Roman alphabet

**FACTS THAT MIGHT BE OVERLOOKED**

**314.** Jesus wasn't a Christian.

**315.** The Milky Way is a galaxy.

**316.** It sounds the same when we say it, but dollars and sense means something different than dollars and cents.

**317.** This moment may be one second, one minute, or it might be an era that is called a moment because time is irrelevant when you are speaking of Eternity.

**318.** You'll never find canned laughter amongst the canned goods at the grocery store.

**319.** Just because something is funny doesn't mean that it is hilarious.

**320.** I've never heard anyone say, 'Surely you gleek,' but gleek is a real word that means jest which also means joke.

**321.** The Founding Fathers of the United States of America are still called revolutionaries and lived at the time of a revolution.

## 322. Nutrition Moment:
## What Do You Crave?

What are you hungry for? Chocolate, spaghetti, meatless chicken quesadillas, perhaps? Don't forget vitamins, minerals, and antioxidants.
We all need water, nutrients and physical food to nourish our human bodies, but what about food for our minds and our souls?

## 323. More *Food For Thought:* money and greed

How can one really be obsessed with money and greed? Is it for the purpose of power, and power over others? Wanting to buy material things for temporary satisfaction? Isn't it much more meaningful, significant and relevant to crave compassion and caring for our fellow human beings and for all life on this beautiful Earth planet? Why would a handful of people want to be greedy and crave access to the vast majority of the whole planet's wealth and resources?

Everyone on the planet makes the world go around, not just a few. We must snap out of complacency and denial and become engaged in the awakening of our genuine purpose on this planet... the total.. the whole... must benefit not just a few.

## 324. SPOILED

There are some who say that westerners and Americans (referring to U.S. Americans) are often very materialistic and very spoiled. You know the expression... spare the rod and spoil the child. There is definitely a big difference between discipline and abuse of a child. Many people grew up taking many things for granted, too. There are varying degrees of that as well I think.

That word spoiled reminds of me of milk... when that spoils it gets nasty. Spoiled brats of any age are like spoiled milk. Don't throw the baby out with the bath water, but for goodness sakes throw out that bath water... NOW!

**325.** How could someone have only negative things to say about something that, in my view and experience, has so many good things about it?

**326.** I never claim to be a perfect human (what an oxymoron that is, right?) or holier than thou, but there are so many human beings that don't treat other human beings with respect and compassion. Whatever happened to acknowledging the Golden Rule, the *treat someone like you want to be treated* rule?

**327.** Give someone a genuine compliment today. There really is no other type of compliment. The so-called disingenuous compliment isn't a compliment at all, it's just lame.

**328.** NOW for a genuine compliment. You have a beautiful Soul... whether you recognize that or not.

### 329. Mirages Are Illusions
I remember driving down many rural and desert roads and seeing what looked to be patches or puddles of water on the pavement ahead. It looked to be maybe 300 to 500 feet ahead and when the car actually reached where that spot would be, there would not be any water there at all. It was a mirage. Those experiences always stay with me and confirm that we cannot judge by appearances. Appearances are misleading.

### 330. Explore the Commons
When we consider what we all have in common, it can make a complex idea easier to begin understanding. What are the commons? They are resources of all kinds that are and can be available to all. Some examples are community projects such as gardens, time banks, free access to the Internet, and online university courses.

### 331. Personhood
I've heard that corporations are the same as persons when it comes to political campaign financing. What? How can a business entity with a board of directors and stock that usually

conducts business in a building be considered a living breathing human being?

If that is true, what about the gender? How can you tell if a corporation is a woman or a man?

### 332. MORE HOLIDAYS
I think that there should be more official Holidays. Do you have some ideas? Here's a list of possible suggestions.

Happy Day, Smile Day, Treat Yourself To A Treat Day, Tesla Day, Artists Day, Your Favorite Musician Day, International Day of Love, Peace and Joy, March Protest Day, April Showers Day, May Flowers Day, First Day of Summer Eve, Halloween in July, Bonus Vacation Day, International Picnic Day, Giving Thanks Day, International Silly Day, Day For Everyone That Doesn't Have a Holiday Named After Them But Should, and Occupy A Holiday.

Add some of your own ideas:

### 333. UNIVERSITY OF THE ETERNAL NOW
The Internet is the campus and all subjects and all levels of
education continue to find their ways into the cyber libraries.
What would you like to focus on next? If in doubt, the
common sense course is always a great way to start.

**334.** Do you know your rights? Well, do you?

**335.** I don't like to say, don't be sad, but I will say don't
remain sad indefinitely.

**336.** I may say 'be happy' to someone, but really just when it
looks like it would lift that someone's spirits.

### 337. CONTENT IS PRIORITY
When producing something of true value, content is more
important than production value and that is not to belittle
production value. It's just when production value is considered
more important than content, then obviously the priorities are
out of order.

### 338. OPPOSITES
Have you ever noticed how many things in our human
experience seem to be articulated or acted upon in opposite
ways of what at the very least makes more sense in reality?

Here are a few examples:

A businessman talks about how freezing pay increases and
forcing other cutbacks are necessary for the employees, yet
doesn't offer to take a personal cut in salary and perhaps even
gives himself a pay raise in addition.

A corporate executive complains about paying more taxes in
general, yet financially benefits from loopholes and subsidies
that are funded by tax dollars.

A spouse says they married for love and later files for divorce
seeming very obsessed with getting money, property, and

material things out of the settlement regardless of what else had been going on in the relationship.

A successful person in general is defined with an assumption that they are moral, ethical, hardworking, etc., whether or not that is actually the case yet if a person seems to be struggling economically, then something is automatically wrong with their character and behavior which is then identified as exclusively synonymous with failure.

**Do you use more than 10% of your brain?**

**339. Contemplation 24: CHILL**
Relax and cool down... get into that mind set...NOW! (No refrigeration necessary)

**340.** I want to love you to the Nth degree because it feels so natural. Like beauty is more than skin deep, it isn't just physical. We have a special bond. It doesn't matter what you call it. So simple, yet complex, like a puzzle every piece has a fit.
*From "Fun (To the Nth Degree)"– NOWMAN's theme song*

**341.** Even when your physical body feels cold, you can still keep your heart warm.

**342. INTEGRATION (More on the Commons)**
It is a good idea to integrate ideas of like-minded individuals that are also interested in collective activities such as utilizing the commons... land, air, food, ecosystems, clothing, shelter, and other shared resources available for the common good.

**343.** Climb to the top of a mountain. Surf like a superman. Make yourself a dream home. Make some career plan. Travel around the world. Read a stimulating book. Be passionate about each day. Create a brand new look. Open up to someone who is special to you, knowing that this one feels the same way, too.
*From "Fun (To the Nth Degree)"- NOWMAN's theme song*

**344. THE NOW MOVEMENT**
This is the movement of everything that moves in the present moment. Pay attention to it right now and you'll understand the experience of living in the present moment.

**345.** You can only be present in the moment 100%. In the present moment, there isn't any greed, but you do have to recognize that everyone who is conscious is aware that they are living in the present moment. There are no special treatments. We are all ONE CONSCIOUS BEING in this very moment NOW!

You Are
**NOW**
R E A D I N G
this
B u t t o n

## 346. THE HOW MOVEMENT

This movement is inspired by the cognition of the importance of HOW the what and why are integrated and put into action. For example, when you create a project aimed at achieving a goal to make something good happen, you focus on the HOW once you determine the what and the why you think that this goal must be accomplished. The end result is of great significance, so HOW you get there requires some contemplation and consideration before it is actively initiated.

## 347. An Activist Superhero

I am actively alive. I am actively writing at the moment; typing words into a document. I can call myself an activist super hero. The world will be a better place because we are all active, in other words, being activists and not de-activists.

## 348. THE *GET OFF YOUR BUTT NOW* MOVEMENT

Don't get stuck in the bottom end or at the rear of life..... Get moving NOW!.....*but* no excuses!

## 349. GAMING

Supposedly there are statistics that indicate that gamers around the globe spend millions of hours a day playing video and online games. I was watching a talk from a video game designer who said that there is a great misunderstanding about gamers obsessed with this pastime. Yes, they could be reading books, and the truth is that many of them probably do read books. The interesting discovery is that gamers are very focused and are very optimistic when they succeed and excel at completing a specific monumental task in the virtual fantasy world.

What if those amazing achievements could be somehow attached to reality where it allows players to achieve outstanding accomplishments in the real world and also actually solve problems? Even some economists are starting to recognize that maybe the focus of playing games and accomplishing goals could mean that there are skills that can be used likewise in the real world with amazing results.

## 350. The Commons: Back To the Basics

We all share the resources of air. We all feel the warmth of the sun. The ground is the same for all of us that stand, walk and run on it. We all used to share clean drinking water. We all must learn to share more of the diversity of resources as a global community.

## 351. OPEN SOURCE

When there is a situation that allows for a lot of spontaneity and a lot of input so long as the content stays true to the integrity of the subject matter or the thing itself, we call that inclusion, and it is open source. It usually refers to some kind of learning experience, but the meaning can be flexible and spontaneous because the source of learning must remain open.

### 352.  ENTERING A NEW ERA MEANS…..

more and more people in the world are waking up and when paying attention there are a lot of signs to indicate that. Revelation is still a process though, so while awareness is raised and good intentions abound, complacency can still be a dominating practice of the status quo.

### 353.  Rhyming Fun

Disrupt the corrupt.   Don't be coy with your joy.   Sow what you flow.

### 354.  Flow of Consciousness

A stream of consciousness flows like the water in an active stream or waterfall.  Don't trickle what you give. Let it gush always!

### 355.  What is EVIL supposed to be anyway?

Evil is actually Live spelled backwards.  When we emphasize evil we are misunderstanding how backwards our thinking can be sometimes.

### 356.  What is good and what is Good?

When a writer uses capital letters, it often means that the author is emphasizing a distinction of some kind unless the word in discussion just happens to be grammatically at the beginning of a sentence.

The distinction that I often make is between Reality and illusion. Illusion can be defined as appearance of Reality, but nothing more. In other words, there is no duality really. Duality is an illusion.

Okay, that is out of the way.  NOW, what is really important to remember here?   Good is at the core of what is REAL (however that REAL manifests Itself).

### 357. The Commons and Common Ground....

As like-minded individuals find each other and meet in person, online or in some other way, a collective forms. The collective also consists of building relationships with individuals and then forming a collective intelligence through dialogue, sustainable projects, and shared resources. In some circles, collective intelligence is linked to HOW the commons is understood by those that share those spaces, scenarios and other tangible resources. Of course resources are not limited to what is considered material. Each individual is essential to the completeness of the commons and we all experience the commons on some level every day. Does it sound complex? Keep it simple and focus on common ground, or in other words, what we all have in common.

### 358. CONTEMPLATION 25
Sanity

In a quiet space, stay focused on sanity even when it seems that the world around you, in your community or region, country or the Earth itself is in some kind of chaos. Contemplation is actually an Eternal never-ending exercise.

## 359. NOWism

Have we made changing hearts and minds a new priority in our lives? Here's a new acronym that I created with actor Jason Alexander. **MDKI** which stands for Meet, Discuss, Create Something, Implement. Did you get the jist of that? It was what came out of a moment of spontaneous collaboration. Remember, all that exists is right NOW... and a moment from NOW.

Comedy Corner

360. The Edutainment Mission

## The Four E's

*Entertainment* serves at least several primary purposes. The obvious one is that it can produce a lot of FUN. In addition though, while it draws attention to relevant issues that are important to many people, it can act as a catalyst for needed change as it provides some temporary relief from the difficult challenges in our ever-evolving society and globalized world.

*Education* is a process that intellectually articulates subject matter and serves as motivation for learning. In addition to what we may call traditional schooling and schools, for instance, focused working groups can also use critical analysis and other effective methods to organize around specific concerns thus creating a highly functional learning environment.

*Edutainment* is the obvious combination of entertainment and education. This not only combines the two words, but actually becomes part of the vernacular of a new and ever evolving culture that not only keeps us informed and proactive as productive global citizens in our local and regional communities, but also serves to *Enlighten* and inspire us to be responsible caretakers of our internal as well as external environments. It is an integration of ideas as well as the unique and functional vehicle for a collective to produce outstanding content that is entertaining, informative and engaging as we together create a new sustainable culture and economy as well as a real global society that is all -inclusive.

LET'S HAVE SOME FUN!

## 361. THE UNIVERSE FROM THE UNIVERSE'S PERSPECTIVE

It's amazing to me that human beings would actually claim that they can actually try to thoroughly and accurately analyze the Universe from the standpoint of the human experience. The human experience tries to explain the Universe from an Earth perspective because as far as we know, no human on this blue planet (as we call it) even the economically wealthiest folks, have not ventured out to other planets as of the moment that I am writing this. Either way, space traveler or not, wouldn't one have to really grasp the immeasurable enormity of the immensity of the Universe, even just speaking of Infinity and Eternity alone?

I am ok with the idea that I don't know what the Universe is all about, but then again, maybe we all really do know what the Universe is just by recognizing the simple fact that the Universe is everything.

I do challenge anyone who wants to seriously try to describe the full essence of the Universe from a limited Earth bound and humanly restricted perspective.

Even in Galileo's day, for instance, the kings and the queens wanted their subjects to believe that the Earth is not only what our sun revolved around, but was also at the center of the Universe itself. Maybe they even wanted to believe that they themselves personally were at the center of the Universe. Galileo and other astronomers knew the truth, but were censored.

In the same way, we can imagine almost anything is true. Imagining something is real or true doesn't automatically mean that it is. It would make sense that the only way to truly understand the Universe would be to know the Universe from the Universe's perspective.

### 362. CONTEMPLATION 26: The Universe Itself

When I contemplate the Universe, what comes to mind is an open, unlimited, unrestricted entity, substance or whatever can actually genuinely manifest. Somehow on some level without words, that description, even that partial definition still resonates with me.

How can the Universe show favoritism towards certain people? How could it regard a certain kind of work as being more important than another kind of work? It doesn't reward or acknowledge actions or labor solely based on some kind of economic system.

The human perspective is just like an opinion, a hypothesis, or perhaps like a theory, but the one fact is so much simpler than that. The Universe just IS. Consider that for a while if you haven't already.

### 363. More on the subject of BACK TO THE BASICS

Everyone needs food, water, air, gravity so that they are grounded.... and happiness should be a necessity as well!

### 364. THE NEW SUPERHERO IN TOWN

Do you know what it is like being the new kid in town? The new 'kid' has to learn so many new names, new routines, new directions to get from place to place, etc. Practically every part of life and the day –to –day experience is new so it takes time to make adjustments. It isn't unusual to be excluded and marginalized even by others with good intentions because the new kid 'isn't from the area' that he or she now calls home.

As the new kid while growing up literally as a child (in biological years), there are usually not reliable and especially on–going mentoring relationships outside of the nuclear family for that same reason, so the new kid often has to learn how to depend on oneself at least in social situations if a stronger support system doesn't seem to exist.

The advantage is that it is more difficult for the new kid to become complacent with the less familiar surroundings yet by also having fewer routines or habits (originating through one's surroundings) than others who have lived in the same neighborhood or area their entire lives, there can often be an extra strong drive to succeed as well.

A whole book can be written on this subject.

It certainly keeps one on their toes, so-to-speak. The new superhero is like the innovator or the visionary that always finds oneself in a unique yet very humbled position.

## 365. WE'RE ALL SUPERHEROES

There have been so many superheroes before me and there are also many who don't wear uniforms or costumes with capes or have the ability to fly through the air.  They are all saving the world somehow though.  That's what a superhero is all about. I guess flying looks impressive, but it is only one way to get from one point to another.

When we wake up and realize that this human Earth experience isn't all about ourselves, we want to *change the world*, impact the lives of others and experience some heaven on Earth, so-to-speak.

At the end of the night, we're all superheroes.

**POSTSCRIPT, EPILOGUE, and all that comes at the end of a book:**

**WE ARE ALL ONE !**


The Earth planet is an amazing yet strange place. While there are many beautiful souls and amazing technologies, stunning terrains and awesome blue skies, there are also mindless behaviors that appear to be destroying the social and physical environments. There are humans treating each other with little or no value and even viewing themselves with such exaggerated high regard or low self-esteem that it makes absolutely no sense whatsoever.

I remind myself daily of the vastness of the Universe. As I often say, there are no limitations and restrictions in the Universe. It is impossible to put boundaries of any kind around it. It is also impossible for it to separate Itself from itself. It must be Intelligence and Perfection in constant Action being everywhere simultaneously forever.

EVERYONE of us together makes up the complete consistency of the Universe. We are Consciousness substance in forms. It really is true when speaking in terms of the Universe that WE ALL ARE ONE!
And of course... ALL THAT EXISTS IS RIGHT NOW!

Even though it is now supposedly the end of this book, it really isn't. You can go back to the beginning and start all over again. There really is no beginning or end that way. You just keep going... this is what we do.

If something or someone in this life gets you down, you don't know what to do or to say, as a friend once said.... and she lived to be over 100 years old in so-called Earth years.

***Keep on keeping on!***

The TRUTH is that we are all essential to the completeness of the vastly beautiful Universe.... **NOW!**

**NISWANDER MUSIC IS AVAILABLE:**

**LD1**
**"Revolution of the Heart" featuring**
Surfin' With Jesus, Funky Space, Chameleon, Touch, Compassion, Anyone Home?, Out of Order, and more!

**LD2**
**"Adventures In Wanderland" featuring the NOWMAN theme song**
Fun (To the Nth Degree), also Read A Book, Everyone, Mojo, The Poet Speaks,
Hats, I've Got To Love You This Way, and more plus the promo movie 'Chameleon.'

CDs and digital downloads available through

CD Baby (go to www.cdbaby.com/niswander1 and www.cdbaby.com/niswander2)

and iTunes.

**WHAT PRESS SAYS ABOUT NISWANDER:**

"With 'Surfin' With Jesus,' he can rely on a single tune to consistently bring down the house."

"Niswander, who fuses a shiny wardrobe with 1980's synthesizer pop to a social conscience and novelty lyrics, disarms the most jaded listeners.  He sings about teenagers who meet aliens, and the crowd loves it."  *(Regarding 'Revolution of the Heart')*

"'Read A Book,' a slab of buzz-saw punk that celebrates literature."

"…music to charm listeners from age 6 to 60."  *(Regarding 'Adventures In Wanderland')*

"If you have any sense of humor, you're in for an unforgettable evening."

**David Lindquist- pop music writer- Indianapolis Star**

"A multi-talented musician" - **Troy Brownfield- Shotgun Reviews (from Indianapolis Monthly Magazine)**

"The genius of Niswander is that nobody quite knows where he is coming from....Is he full of energy and wit? Undoubtedly. Is he a great stage presense? Definitely."

*Regarding 'Revolution of the Heart':* "An album that's for the most part, catchy and intriguing." **Steve Hammer- Nuvo Newsweekly**

" Niswander is what a lot of musicians are not these days: a true entertainer... He tells us stories of his life and love of characters. The songs are good-natured and dreamy, heart-felt and performed with passion." **Harmonie- Nuvo Newsweekly**

**If you could pick any Hoosier act (besides John Mellencamp!) to perform at the Super Bowl halftime show, who would it be?**

**Artist: Niswander**
**(Joey 'Fingers' Montgomery- General Manager- Metromix-Indianapolis)**
**2011**

# EXTRAS

# CREATION.

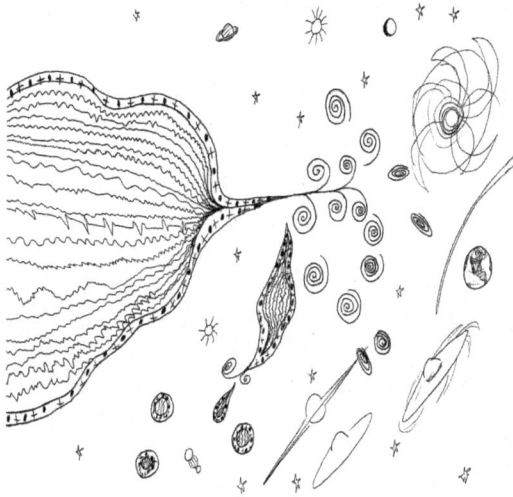

When all that exists is the Present Moment, how can there be creation which implies a beginning that happened before or will happen after....the Eternal NOW?

**LEND ME YOUR EARS.**

**It is impossible to actually borrow someone's ears. This metaphor obviously means listen to what is verbalized.**

**The Atomic Structure.**

THE ATOMIC
STRUCTURE

The atomic structure consists of a bunch of particles that can never be completely broken down to a smallest size because the substance of the particles is Infinite. It is like trying to limit NOW and Eternity with a measurement of time or limit the Universe Itself.

**One Life.**

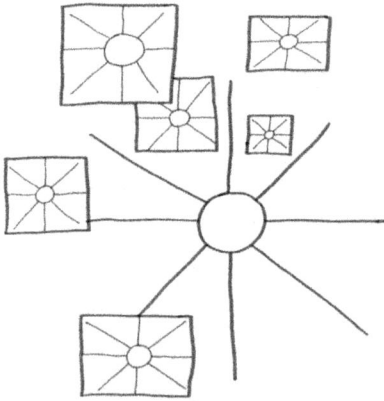

ONE Life, ONE cause,
ONE effect, ONE
Radiating LIFE.

Here and NOW, we are aware that we are conscious of One Life.  We just know that it is what it is...even when we don't use words to describe it.  We just know.

**Occupy The Soapbox.**

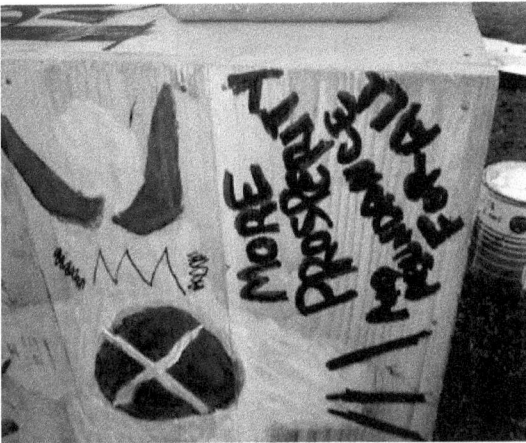

The purpose of a soapbox is to stand on it and speak to crowds about what is on your mind. I painted on this soapbox "More Prosperity and Abundance For All".... Let it happen NOW!

**Make A Big Splash!**

**Draw attention to something truly significant NOW!**

**Beep Beep.**

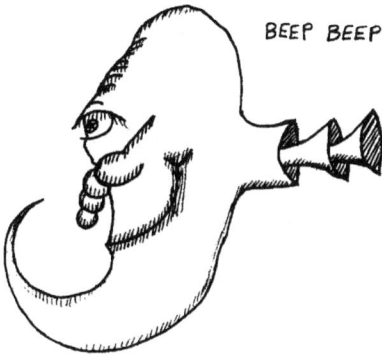

BEEP BEEP

**Sometimes you just have to blow your own horn..... or something like that.**

**Three Heads Are Better Than One.**

'Three's a crowd' is the famous expression. What it really means is that we all exist together NOW on this Earth planet.

**The Yin and Yang of Magnetism.**

**The attraction is automatic and same-mindedness is like a magnet that naturally draws us together.**

This is.... Very Strange.

**VERY
STRANGE**

Sometimes when something is misunderstood, not familiar, or even perceived as weird, it is often called strange. Why is that?  It is just as easy to say that something believed to be normal could also be perceived as strange.

**This way....**

**Kite.**

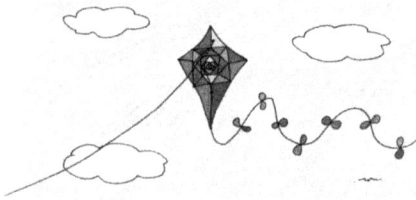

**Flying a kite has always fascinated curious minds. It represents the constant calm and happy-go-lucky existence of a free spirit.**

**Geo Space.**

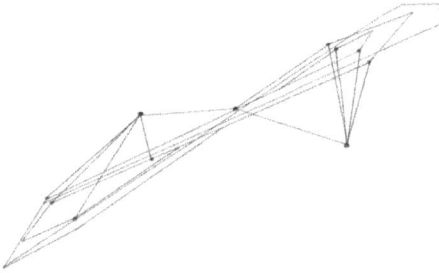

**Abstract art defies the conventional, but it leaves much room for the imagination.**

**The Door Is Open....**

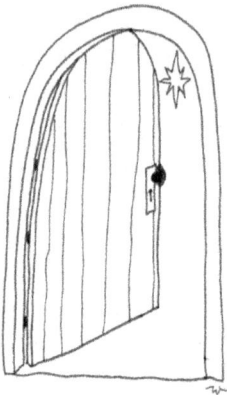

**The open door represents new opportunities and adventures. Carpe diem!**

**NOW!**

**Notes:**

www.ingramcontent.com/pod-product-compliance
Lightning Source LLC
Chambersburg PA
CBHW071536040426
42452CB00008B/1042